Black Girl in
MOSCOW,
A Memoir

Black Girl in
MOSCOW,
A Memoir

JACQUELINE CLAY CHESTER

authorHOUSE®

AuthorHouse™
1663 Liberty Drive
Bloomington, IN 47403
www.authorhouse.com
Phone: 1-800-839-8640

Published by AuthorHouse   11/26/2014

ISBN: 978-1-4969-2479-7 (sc)
ISBN: 978-1-4969-2478-0 (hc)
ISBN: 978-1-4969-2477-3 (e)

Library of Congress Control Number: 2014911972

Dedicated to God Most High.
To my mother, Emma E. Martin; son, Scott Chester and his wife, Evelyn; daughter, Rachel Vassel, and son-in-law, Don Vassel; son, Capt. Shawn Chester; brother Atty. Henry Clay; grandchildren, Arielle, Victoria, Chase, and Alexandra; family and friends Susann, Ron, Anita, Debra; Juanita, Vincent, Millie, Freddie, and archivist, Kevin Sipp and Morris Gardner; plus anyone I pinned into a corner to read passages from my books,
Thank You!

INTRODUCTION

Do you believe in omens?

Six years before I ever heard of the American National Exhibition in Moscow, and six years before I ever knew I'd embark on a six thousand mile journey behind the Iron Curtain, and six years before I ever dreamed I would be one of forty-seven models on an outdoor stage in a park called "Sokolniki," modeling before thousands of Russian men, women and children, I believe I had received an omen. I was fifteen years old then, and I lived with my parents in Brooklyn, New York.

Monday through Friday, I traveled the New York City subway system to attend school in Manhattan. One morning, as I walked along the subway platform, I was strongly impacted by newspaper headlines that fairly screamed, "Joseph Stalin, Leader of the Soviet Union Is Dead!"

I admit I knew little of Joseph Stalin. I knew of course that he was the leader of the Soviet Union, and therefore a huge figure on the world stage. But suddenly the life of this man captured my imagination. For reasons unbeknownst to me, I purchased newspapers and began reading every article about Stalin and the country he had ruled. I read and filed away stories about his life and his rise to leadership in the Union of Soviet Socialist Republics (USSR). I studied photographs of him as he appeared as a young man and as he reached maturity, but why? I had no classes in Russian history or literature that required this kind of diligence. As a result I felt acquiring this information, served no real purpose. But then surprisingly, as time went on, I discovered I had learned more about this Russian dictator and his country than any crash course could offer.

Article after article revealed that as Stalin grew in power, so did his ruthlessness. Hands down and bar none Stalin deservedly won the title of the Mass Murderer of the Century. During his reign he executed eight to twenty million of his own countrymen. Even those who considered themselves his friend found themselves standing before a firing squad. Seemingly Stalin took demonic pleasure in pitting married couples against each other, eventually executing both, leaving their families bereft and shattered. Stalin would even execute his personal doctors if they displeased him.

In photographs, before she took her life, his young wife smiled happily with Stalin by her side. There were photographs of Stalin posing affectionately with his daughter Svetlana. To Svetlana, Stalin was known only as her adoring father, but what did she feel when she finally learned he was the murderer of millions?

Through these newspaper accounts, I learned about the Russian people and how many suffered under Stalin's rule. My seemingly aimless quest had inadvertently increased my overall knowledge about this country and its people.

But on the morning of March 1, 1953, it was noted that Stalin had not exited his dacha. Everyone knew it was unusual for him to sleep late but no one dared take the chance on disturbing him. Through that morning and into the afternoon, Stalin's door remained shut. But the day wore on and so although fearful of Stalin's vile temper his attendants bravely entered his cabin. Stalin was found on the floor beside his bed. He had suffered a stroke and was seriously ill. It was clear, during those critical hours, Stalin had struggled to live. Doctors he had imprisoned were consulted to try and save his life. But, the atmosphere of fear was so pervasive, in the end it cost Stalin his life.

Although my knowledge of Russia had increased, I had no intention to visit this faraway country, but life had other plans for my future. Six years later, I found myself sitting on a plane that was making its way toward Russia's capital city of Moscow.

At the time, I thought there was nothing unusual about my being a black girl in Moscow. Of course now I realize Russia, especially during the Cold War, was indeed a unique destination for an African American female or perhaps any American to take. But then, if I had listened carefully, I would have realized this trip was foretold by an omen years ago.

TABLE OF CONTENTS

CHAPTER 1

Who Are Russians?

As an American black girl in Moscow, my position was unique, and among the Russians, I was a rare girl indeed. I came from a position of strength with a mighty country behind me and therefore a definitive culture woven into the fabric of my being. Educated, smart, and savvy, I had not simply stumbled onto Russian shores; I came with knowledge about my host country and brought my Western know-how to share.

But the question might be, do people of color live among the fair-skinned or white people of Russia? To think of Russia as a country having a biracial population might be difficult for some, but although small in number, there is a percentage of biracial people, or Afro-Russians, to whom Russia is home. The descendants of these biracial individuals left their native lands, traveled to Russia, and settled there. Their offspring, brown in color, know no country but Russia and speak no language but Russian. Genghis Kahn invaded Russia centuries ago, but his DNA is still evident today. Every so often, on a street in Moscow, you will see a white Russian with natural blond hair and blue or brown eyes. But take a closer look; that individual's facial features are clearly Asian, consisting of the hooded eyes, full lips, and high cheekbones.

Alexander Pushkin, the proclaimed Russian literary genius, was of mixed race. Alexander's great-grandfather on his mother's side arrived in Russia shackled in chains as a slave from Africa. But during his lifetime, this slave raised himself to the ranks of a Russian nobleman. Slightly more than a generation or so later, this former slave (now a Russian nobleman) has a great-grandson who at the age of fifteen published his first poem. The poem received much acclaim, and young Pushkin was hailed a genius. Pushkin later became the founder of modern Russian literature.

From my very first week in Moscow, I was so embraced by the Russian people that I gave very little thought to being a black girl in Moscow. I was dined and escorted to various concerts, ballets, operas, symphonies, museums, and parties at several consulates. I think I was considered a rare and special import from America by the men I dated, and the brown hue of my skin did not seem to be an issue. Interracial dating was still taboo in most of America in the late 1950s, and marriage was banned in most states. In Russia, marriage between mixed couples might be a tenuous affair but was not illegal. I learned later that race relations in Russia had layers of concerns that were not always evident to the casual foreign visitor.

We Americans brought the American National Exhibition in Moscow to Russia, but Russian newspapers declared that the Soviet people had little or no interest in things American. So as workmen put the finishing touches on the eleven acres of Sokolniki Park, where the American National Exhibition in Moscow would take place, we Americans had no idea if we would be welcomed or not. The Cold War was not over, and an entire decade had been spent stockpiling weapons to destroy. Would a well-meaning group of Americans erase the memory of those competitive years? Taking a serious look, the American National Exhibition in Moscow seemed a huge gamble.

Bi-racial, Alexander Pushkin, became the founder of
Modern Russian Literature

CHAPTER 2

My Metamorphosis

Would I have been ready for such an amazing trip had I not had major good fortune earlier? My first stroke of good luck was attending my all-girls junior high school in Harlem, New York. For a brief period, my family and I lived in Harlem. We moved back to Brooklyn, but I never changed schools. So every school day, I took the subway train from Norstrand Avenue in Brooklyn to 125th Street in Harlem, a trip that took about forty minutes. I then walked from 125th Street to 119th to Junior High School 81. But once inside the walls of that school, each girl blossomed—at least, I felt I did. My teachers made me realize I had the ability to express myself on paper. I was always chosen to read my book reports or compositions in my English classes.

Then one day, Mrs. Hyman, my English teacher, told me I could be a writer if I wanted to. As I stood before her, I swelled with pride but was too shy to ask how one might begin. But her belief in me lifted my spirits and made me grow emotionally.

Other teachers encouraged my painting. From a very young age, I would draw on brown paper bags my parents brought home from the grocery store. I would flatten the bags out and use them as drawing paper.

At home, drawing was just something I did, but at school, my teachers called my ability to draw talent.

Of all the creative things I enjoyed, singing was my passion. I think back now on our glee club of thirty African American girls. We were introduced to music outside of the contemporary music we listened to. We all felt the passion of the lyrics in the Scottish love song "Annie Laurie": "Her brow is like the snowdrift, her throat is like a swan and her face, it tis the fairest that ere the sun shone on!"

With voices at perfect pitch, we dove into that divine melody, encouraged by our teacher, who was also our maestro. While holding her baton, she flung her arms skyward, driving us, commanding us onward as we ascended towards a crescendo of sound, bringing the song to its brave conclusion: "And for bonnie Annie Laurie, I'd lay me doone and dee!"

Who Annie Laurie was was not important; we were simply elated at being pushed to our limits and discovering how our young voices could make sweet music. The song was a journey of self-discovery as our voices boldly rose like the tentative roar of lion cubs.

I grew intellectually in junior high school, but the physical side of me was dismaying. When I compared myself to my classmates, I had no curves; I was too skinny. I thought I had the body of a teenage boy. The girls in my class, thirteen- and fourteen-year-olds, were budding. They had hips, breasts, and a little saunter when they walked. How I wanted to mimic their way of walking. I realized that to walk like them, I needed to have all the other components—the hips, heavy thighs, jutting breasts, and a whole lot of attitude. I felt I lacked everything they had in abundance, and I didn't think there was any way I'd ever catch up.

I graduated from junior high and I continued my education at Charles Evans Hughes High School in the borough of Manhattan. Immediately, I realized my school in Harlem provided an intimacy with teachers and classmates that my new school did not. I missed that intimacy.

Charles Evans Hughes was located on West 18th Street and 8th Avenue and had a huge student population that was 75 percent white with the remaining 25 percent being African American, Hispanic, and Asian. The other equation was that Hughes was co-ed. It was an adjustment to share a classroom with boys. But all went well, and I made friends and adjusted.

In my second year at Hughes, the Student Council decided to have a school-wide beauty contest. Four sophomore girls were to be nominated by the students as candidates for this contest. Then every student would vote on which of the four would carry that esteemed title of Ms. Charles Evans Hughes.

I was knee-deep in homework and various school projects, and I hardly had a minute to think about the contest. It was entertaining but seemed a waste of time when there was so much to do. Memories of my junior high years when I was unhappy with my looks might have had something to do with how I viewed this contest. Those years when I felt I didn't measure up physically still haunted me. I was also now attending a school whose white population was the majority, and the school had its share of pretty white girls.

But although I didn't feel a part of such a contest, the excitement it caused was contagious, and every once in a while, I'd take note of the latest candidate. One nominee was an Irish girl named Mira Fair. She and I had a few classes together, and I liked her. To me, her name alone seemed a description of who she was. She was a fair maiden, you might say—pretty, with a charming smile; short, curly brown hair; a neat, slender figure; great clothes; and a pleasing personality. I thought with all she had going for her, how could she lose?

I waited to see who else would be nominated, but so far, Mira Fair had my vote. But life in high school was never predictable, and wonders of wonders, a few days later, yours truly was nominated as one of the four candidates!

I had to ask myself a question or two. Since junior high, had I somehow changed? Was I an ugly duckling back then who had somehow morphed into a swan? But what the heck? Suddenly I was wildly excited that I had been nominated at all. Perhaps I had somehow pulled the wool over someone's eyes, but I wasn't going to worry; being nominated was more than this skinny Brooklyn girl could have hoped for. With the four nominated candidates, campaigning now began in earnest.

Posters lined the walls in the cafeteria and halls. There was energy in the activities of the students that was hard not to feel. Everyone from students to teachers to cafeteria workers was excited about the contest. The excitement traveled like a train, down the corridors, through the classrooms, and bounced off the walls of the stairwells. The excitement was electrifying! The day finally arrived when students had to cast their ballots. I was the only black candidate running against three attractive white female students. The contest in itself had been fun, and if nothing else, I could live with that.

The voting process went quickly. After every ballot had been counted, the winner was announced. "Who?" I stared at Mr. Dombrow, the principal. I was on the verge of hyperventilating as I listened to what he was telling me. "Are you sure?" I asked, not quite understanding that students—white, black, brown, red, and yellow—had overwhelmingly voted for me. Mr. Dombrow smiled reassuringly. "I won?" I asked again, making sure I'd gotten it right.

"Yes, you won. Your fellow students voted for you."

Well, I didn't know what to do with myself. Why hadn't I practiced being a winner? Well, I never expected to win!

My first thought was to make it home as fast as I could. I was sure my mother wouldn't believe this either! I ran the four blocks to the subway and stood on the platform, waiting for the train. All the while, I wondered, *Are they sure? Did I hear him right?* Maybe there was to be another vote, a final vote. No, no final vote; I had won! "Mom!" I called as I burst through the downstairs door. I ran by twos up the stairs, down the hall, and into the kitchen. "Mom, guess what?" My mother was standing at the sink. "Can you believe it? Mom, pinch me and tell me I'm not dreaming!"

I looked at my mother, perfectly sure I would never in my whole life deliver more astonishing news! "Mom," I said as I took a deep breath, "I won!" Wide-eyed, I looked to her for a response. I actually believed she would tell me there had been an error. Maybe she had received a phone call from the principle saying he had made a mistake. But she was silent; her silence forced me to go on. "I was voted, Ms. Charles Evans Hughes!" I proclaimed this great news as though I had found a trillion dollars in a box of Cracker Jacks.

Perhaps she too was stunned and didn't know how to respond. But she did not grab me to ply me with hugs, kisses, or words of congratulations. Was I expecting too much? Without the reaction I expected from her, I decided on my own that in winning, I might consider the possibility that I was perhaps pretty, a little bit. I was suddenly forced to see myself as I thought others must see me—skinny or not—and whether my mother said so or not, I had to believe I perhaps wasn't half bad to look at.

CHAPTER 3

My Mother's Philosophy

Nothing more was said by my mother or stepfather about my being the winner of the contest that had turned my world upside down. That evening, my mother, stepfather, and I sat at the table together and had a quiet dinner. Afterward, I washed the dishes as my parents went to bed.

For a country girl from rural Georgia, my mother had a highly developed sense of style and fashion. She might have been born in rural Georgia, but New York City was where she belonged! Living in New York City, she learned about fashion, fine jewelry, home décor, and much more. She seemed born to appreciate and recognize beauty, quality, and style. Everyone in our family knew that to receive a gift from my mother was to receive a gift that was quality and uniquely suited to the individual she had purchased it for. It was always the right size, your most becoming color, and the style that would suit you best.

My mother was not much of a talker. Once in a while, she would tell me of some incident that took place when she was a girl in the south. Times were hard for her father as he attempted to make a living as a sharecropper. As one of eight children, until the age of seven, my mother had never owned anything that had not first been worn by one or all of her siblings. But fortune smiled on her one day when a family friend gave her a brand new pair of socks. It wasn't much in the way of a gift, but it was the first new item of clothing she had ever owned.

She loved those socks. Each time she wore them, she would later wash them and let them dry in the sun on the clothesline in the back yard. When they were dry, she would fold then and put them safely away until she needed to wear them again. But one day, she went to take them off the line, and there was only one and a half socks hanging there. She realized the pet goat had eaten the half that was missing. My mother was devastated and cried for a week!

"A week? Why did you cry so long over a sock?" I asked her.

"Because I knew it would be another three, four, or five years before I'd get anything new again!"

What did it feel like to wait years to get something new and all your own? My mother viewed the situation in her unique way. She decided she had treasured the socks too much. Perhaps without meaning to, she had boasted about them or felt too proud when she wore them. She concluded that perhaps anything she loved too much would eventually be taken away.

Frightened by this conclusion, I believe she decided to take no chances. No words of praise or boasting about something or someone she loved would pass her lips. Even when her only child was born, she could never say what other mothers felt free to say about their daughters: "You are pretty, smart, and I love you." She wasn't going to let vengeful gods hear her speak those words. So I grew up never hearing the words I longed to hear her say; but she showed her abundant love in other ways.

A few days before the all-important official crowning of Ms. Hughes was to take place, my mother brought home a rather large white box. The box was sitting on the kitchen table when I walked in from school. "Hi, Mom." I spotted the box. "What's that?" I asked.

"You can open it," she said nonchalantly as she prepared dinner.

I walked over to the table where the box lay. It smelled new and looked expensive. I carefully removed the string and then gently lifted the lid. I looked down on soft white tissue paper that seemed as delicate as clouds. I pushed the paper aside to see what lay beneath. My heart skipped a beat as I looked down on the most stunning dress I had ever seen in all my seventeen years!

Tenderly and with my heart a-flutter, I lifted the embroidered, creamy yellow silk shantung dress that had lain nestled in the box. "Oh, Mom," was all I could say as I held that gorgeous dress up against my body. "Can

I try it on?" I asked, not believing this beautiful creation was mine. My mother was busy cooking, so she only nodded slightly. I turned and ran into my bedroom.

A few minutes later, I returned, wearing that divine dress. It fit as though it had been tailored to my figure. It had huge puffed sleeves, a flattering square neckline, and the tapered waist hugged my nineteen-inch waistline to perfection.

Its full skirt had yards of crinoline underneath that caused the dress to stand out like an umbrella. When I walked, I appeared to float. I gave no thought to how much money this lovely dress must have cost my parents. I looked over at my mom and was delighted by her shy smile as she eyed her spinning, twirling daughter. Displays of affection were rare in our house, but I couldn't resist giving my mother a quick hug and kiss on her cheek. "How do I look, Mom?" I asked to mask my embarrassment for having impulsively kissed her. Her hands, stirring vegetables in a pot, stopped for a brief second as she appraised me. Characteristically, she finally said, "It will do!"

I marveled at how she seemed to have a collection of phrases that were at best minimal. I had to be satisfied with "It will do" as her strongest form of approval.

Emma E. Martin, my eloquent mother

CHAPTER 4

The Crowning of Ms. Hughes

The official crowning of Miss Charles Evans Hughes took place in the school auditorium on a balmy night in June. Of course, I arrived in my enchanting yellow dress. Unfortunately, things are sticky when you have a modern-day family! At this gala event, my mother and stepfather were present; my biological father had also flown in from Detroit, Michigan to attend. The three met in the school's lobby, but they were obviously uneasy in each other's company. Neither seemed to know what to say to the other. Eye contact was avoided. Didn't they realize they had *me* in common? Could not I have been a subject of conversation for them?

My mother also seemed at a loss for words as she stood between the two men—one who represented her past and the other who represented her future. Meanwhile, there I was among these three adults, but no one said anything like, "That's my girl," perhaps because they did not know who to give credit to for the young girl they were there to celebrate. It was indeed an awkward and uncomfortable moment, but take it or leave it; somehow, we were family!

The doors to the auditorium opened, and my mother and stepfather found seats together while my father sat a few rows away. When it was time for the program to begin, the auditorium was packed with students and their families.

Everyone was seated as I entered the auditorium. There was a distinct hush as all talking ceased and all eyes turned in my direction. Holding my head up high, I steeled my jittery nerves and glided down the aisle to sit next to my mother and stepfather. I felt regal and proud in my magnificent yellow dress.

I pretended not to notice as students turned to look at me to see how I was taking this remarkable evening. I appeared calm but hoped no one could hear my heart pounding in my chest!

Finally, our high school principal, Mr. Dombrow, stepped out on stage. He was a Jewish man of great personal charm. He wore a navy blue suit that was a perfect fit for his slender frame. He was well-liked, and although he could be firm with students who stepped out of line, it was generally known that he was always fair. He received a warm ovation as he stepped up to the microphone and greeted the energized students and their parents. "This is a wonderful night," he began, "and an unusual night. We have come together as a high school and have voted for one student who will represent our school with dignity and pride during the year to come."

Cheers rose from the students. "I am proud of each of you for democratically carrying out the process of voting for our very first Miss Charles Evans Hughes!"

Wild cheers erupted as students applauded each other and felt proud of their participation in the voting process. Then one by one, Mr. Dombrow announced the names of the three students who were the runners-up. As he announced each name, the girl mounted the stage. The students went wild and gave each runner-up enthusiastic applause. The guys in the auditorium cat called and whistled, and everyone laughed.

Mr. Dombrow said, "This room is loaded with progesterone tonight!" The assembly howled again with laughter. Waiting for the students to quiet a little, Mr. Dombrow continued, "Tonight, we come together to welcome and congratulate the girl voted Ms. Charles Evans Hughes. Let's give our beautiful and charming Jacqueline Clay a hand and ask her to come forward."

I rose from my seat and was greeted by ear-splitting whistles, cat calls, and applause. For a second, I held my breath, or perhaps I just wasn't able to breathe.

Students sitting to my left rose from their seats to allow me to make my way to the center aisle. I believe I murmured a little "Thank you" as I passed by.

I walked slowly down the aisle, purposely not wanting to rush this amazing moment. Finally, as I reached the stage, the entire auditorium erupted into more exuberant applause, whistles, and cheers! Students stood, arms waving in the air, as they watched me approach the stage. Whistles, shouts of "Hooray!" roars, and laughter filled the auditorium. I wondered how the very walls kept from shaking!

As I approached the stage, a male student lent me a hand to make sure I mounted the steps without mishap. On stage, I greeted the three lovely runners-up by shaking the hand of each as they greeted me with broad smiles and congratulated me. I walked over to Mr. Dombrow and extended my hand, which he grasped and vigorously shook in a hearty greeting. I finally turned and faced the audience, and there was no way I could not feel the love in that place! I briefly closed my eyes and held my breath, drinking it all in, wanting to fill every fiber of my being with that awesome moment.

As I stood facing the audience, all three runners-up helped in draping a satin, sparkly "Ms. Charles Evans Hughes" banner across my chest. I smiled as I looked down at it and gently touched each sequined letter. The principal joked with me and made me laugh. The students, hearing his jokes, laughed along with us.

Next, Mira Fair graciously handed me a gigantic bouquet of flowers. Looking at my bouquet, I realized each red, yellow, pink, or violet flower seemed to represent every amazing student in that huge auditorium. "Would our newly crowned Ms. Hughes, like to say a word?" Mr. Dombrow asked. It took me a second to realize he was talking to me. I was indeed Ms. Charles Evans Hughes!

Proudly, I stepped up to the microphone, and the auditorium suddenly went quiet. If a pin had dropped, everyone would have heard it fall.

I stood before the microphone and scanned that packed auditorium. "Hi," I said, poised beyond what I would have thought possible had this night have happened a few short years ago.

Everyone shouted back, "Hi!" We all laughed.

"I know how busy we all are with schoolwork and homework and all the stuff in between, but I wanted to thank each and every one of you for taking the time to vote in this amazing contest, for making me Ms. Charles

Evans Hughes! Every vote cast made this beautiful night possible. I love you all. I'll definitely be seeing you around! Thank you, thank you!"

They liked my speech and applauded with enthusiasm.

I stepped away from the microphone and clutched my bouquet of flowers, relieved I had not stumbled over my words. Mr. Dombrow took over again, thanked both students and parents for coming, and wished everyone safe trips home.

Afterward, students mounted the stage and took pictures with me. I smiled and basked in that moment as I received hugs and kisses and many embraces!

Afterwards, some kids I didn't know well asked me to hang out with them. I really wanted to, if for no other reason than to make this wonderful night last a little longer, but my mother was against it.

Strangely, I don't remember if my father and I talked, but I remember feeling slightly sad that he had come so far and I can't remember if we even exchanged a hug. As we stood outside on the sidewalk, I think he said a few hesitant words indicating he had enjoyed the evening. But my last memory was of him waving a brief goodbye, walking away, looking handsome in the way most women would appreciate, and leaving me with my mother and my stepfather. We three then turned and walked to the 14th Street subway station. There we entered and waited for the next train that would take us home.

Peering into the dark tunnel, I saw the bright one-eyed light of the approaching train. Seemingly in slow motion, the train pulled into the station. In one of its windows, I caught my reflection. As the train slowed, I was able to follow the window that held that reflection. When the train finally came to a stop, I checked my reflection for signs of the duck, but the duck was gone. In its place stood the swan, confident and regal, in her beautiful yellow dress, and across her chest was the sequined Ms. Charles Evans Hughes banner that sparkled.

Stepping into the subway car, I found a seat by a window. As the train pulled away, I searched again through the window for the duck. But the duck was no more. Breathing a sigh of relief, I saw my reflection, and there was the swan, clutching her lovely bouquet of flowers. The swan and I settled back as the train pulled out of the station. Briefly, I closed my eyes to give thanks for such a glorious night as our train moved rapidly into the tunnel, taking us home to Brooklyn.

Magical high school moment when I was crowned
Ms. Charles Evans Hughes!

CHAPTER 5

Attending College in the Fashion Capital

I was accepted as a design student at FIT after my graduation from high school. I had also won an art scholarship to the prestigious Art Students League on 57th Street in New York City. My decision was to attend FIT Monday through Friday and Saturday classes at the Art Students League.

I laugh now, thinking of my first class at the Arts Students League. I entered the classroom and was at first struck that the students were of mixed ages. Some of the male students looked to be between thirty and fifty. I took a seat with my art pad and pencils and waited for the teacher to arrive. Each time an adult entered the room, I was sure it was our teacher, but it was always just another student.

Finally, a woman walked in and went straight to the front of the classroom. I watched, and as she placed her handbag on an extra chair, I was sure this was the beginning of her lecture. But instead, she proceeded to take her jacket off, fold it neatly, and place it on top of her handbag. Next, off came her blouse, followed by her bra, skirt, and underpants. Before my eyes, she had removed every stitch of clothing she had worn into the room, including her shoes. I was more than shocked; I was mortified and wondered what kind of school this was. I sat there, embarrassed and hiding behind my eighteen-by-twenty-four-inch drawing pad.

Slowly, I glanced around the classroom to see if anyone else found this woman's behavior bizarre, but to my surprise, they were looking at the woman from different angles like she was an object, and some had even begun drawing her. It was then I realized this class was a life drawing class. I turned back to the woman, who was our model, and began to draw her naked form. In a matter of seconds, my perspective changed. She was no longer a naked woman but a form to study and draw. Light and shadow played off her hair, face, shoulders, and breasts. I had learned my first lesson in art.

The Fashion Institute of Technology was located in midtown Manhattan on 27th Street, fewer than ten blocks from where I had attended high school. FIT lay nestled in the cradle of the New York City's Garment Center and fabulous fashion industry.

The college had an annual fashion show, a big gala event. FIT's Apparel Design students were to submit their most fabulous creations, hoping to have their designs selected for the fashion show. The student designer was then given notice that his or her design had been selected for the show. That designer then had to select a student to model the garment. If a student agreed to become a designer's model, that student must also agree to make time for several fittings as well.

When some students were asked once, I was asked by three design students to be their model in the fashion show, and I couldn't say no. I was busy with my own classwork, but now my schedule included fittings for three student designers. Somehow I managed everything. The evening of FIT's Annual Fashion Show finally arrived. Not only were family members in attendance, but also well-known designers and companies sending scouts to recruit and offer jobs to students. The fashion show was the highlight of the season, and after the show was over, things again settled down.

A few weeks later, I was in my pattern-making class. I had just taken my muslin fabric out and placed my scissors on the table when my professor walked past me and whispered in my ear. "Excuse me?" I said, not sure of what I had heard him say.

"Mrs. Goodman is expecting you in her office within the next twenty minutes. If I were you, I'd not keep her waiting."

"Why?" I asked, but the teacher just strolled away. I wondered why Mrs. Shirley Goodman, liaison secretary of the college, would want to see me. I quickly left the classroom and walked down the hall to the elevator. I pressed the button, and as the doors opened, I stepped inside. I was still trying to think of a reason for being summoned. Had I failed a class? No, I didn't think so. Had my tuition check bounced? No, I doubted that, too.

The elevator doors slid open, and I was on the first floor. I stepped out and hastily walked down the long hallway to Mrs. Goodman's office. Her secretary, an attractive blond named Nancy, greeted me, and in a few minutes, Nancy was escorting me in to see Mrs. Goodman. Her office was spacious and attractive and decorated with the colors beige, pale aqua, and tan. I looked at this distinguished woman sitting behind her desk. I'd seldom seen her in person, but I knew she was involved in several organizations that supported the college. Due to her efforts, the college had grown.

Mrs. Goodman was an attractive woman with natural salt and pepper hair cut in an attractive bob. She wore a fabulous light gray glen plaid suit and was busy going through some papers on her desk but looked up, smiled, and offered me a seat. Nervous, I sat and folded my hands in my lap. "What are your plans for the summer?" Mrs. Goodman asked, still shuffling papers.

"I'll work this summer at A & S's department store," I answered, proud to have secured a summer position.

She smiled and nodded her head. The next question she asked left me speechless. "How would you like to go to Moscow?"

I was too stunned to answer. I'd heard of a town in Idaho called Moscow, and I wasn't really sure how I felt about going to Idaho. But as though she was reading my mind, Mrs. Goodman added, "And I mean Moscow, Russia."

I was not able to say yes fast enough! "Okay," she said, "you'll have to audition Saturday morning at 9:00 a.m. Ask Nancy for the directions."

Everything after that was a blur. I was so elated, I kept thinking, *Moscow, Russia, wow!*

For some reason, I always had an interest in Russian things. How did it happen that in a household where gospel music was heard on our radio more often than not, I loved classical music and many of the Russian composers like Tchaikovsky and Rimsky Korsakov? I was interested in reading articles about Russians who defected to the United States, seeking creative freedom. I felt they were brave to leave the country of their birth to reside in a distant land. Who was not drawn to movies of the Czar, the assassination of his family, and the rumors that their young daughter, Anastasia, had perhaps survived the slaughter?

I remembered a day in junior high school when my teacher lectured our class on Russian history and spoke about Russia's temporary government after the February Revolution in 1917 and then the October Revolution that caused so much hardship for the Russian people. "What was Russia's temporary government called?" our teacher asked the class. There was silence; several minutes passed as she waited for an answer.

I sat, piecing together what she had said about the turmoil the country had experienced. Both Kerensky and Lenin struggled for power, and I knew the Kerensky name, which I connected to the temporary government. I raised my hand. "Provisional was the name of Russia's temporary government," I said. "That provisional or temporary government lasted only about eight months."

My teacher said yes and turned and wrote the words "Provisional Government" on the blackboard. Years later, for reasons unknown, I still remembered that feel good moment as I answered her question in my eighth-grade class.

I took the subway home and dashed up the stairs, knowing that at this time of day, my mother would be in the kitchen, preparing dinner. "Mom, Mom! Guess where I've been asked to spend the summer!" I charged into the kitchen, bursting with excitement and energy. "You'll never guess!" I shouted. The water was running in the sink as my mother rinsed lettuce leaves for her salad. She looked at me and patiently waited for me to give her my latest bit of exciting news, knowing I would fairly burst if I didn't tell her soon. She turned off the water, her hands momentarily resting as she waited. "Mom, FIT has asked me to spend seven weeks in Moscow!"

I don't think she batted an eye. "I would be a model, Mom." I continued, waiting for some reaction from her, "for the American Natural Exhibition in Moscow! Moscow, Russia, Mom!" I reiterated.

She stared at me, weighing my information. Then she turned back to the sink and placed the rinsed lettuce leaves into a large glass bowl. I stood there, hardly believing she wasn't actually fainting. She looked my way again and said, "That's nice. Now set the table for dinner."

When I woke up on Saturday morning, my mother, who hadn't said anything about Moscow, was already in the kitchen, preparing a light breakfast for me. I walked in, still wearing my pajamas, and gave her a quick hug. Hugs were rare for us. Neither one of us seemed to know how to hug comfortably. But because I thought I knew why she had gotten up early, it seemed a hug was in order.

She usually slept late on Saturdays, so I knew she had gotten up early for me. She wanted me to talk to her about the trip to Moscow. She wouldn't ask questions, but she would let me feed her details.

Who was going? (A group of models of various ages and three administrators, including Mrs. Goodman.) How many were going? (Fifty in total.) Where would we stay? (It was arranged that we would stay in a hotel in Moscow.) I talked, and my mother listened. With each answer, I saw her comfort level rise.

Today was the audition, and I explained to her that I was nervous because I really wanted to take this trip to Moscow. "What are you nervous about?" my mother asked confidently. "Just go in there and do your best."

My mother's words were simple and direct, and I felt they revealed her faith in me. My best would be good enough for her, so to her, it should be good enough for them! If I passed or failed, the important thing was that I had done my best. My mother had spoken, and I felt my nervousness slip away.

When I finished the breakfast she had prepared, she wouldn't let me wash my dishes, another indication she wanted me to spend that time getting myself ready for my audition. Although she hadn't said much about this trip to Moscow, her actions and words this morning revealed she wanted me to experience this unique opportunity.

I took my shower and stood looking in the mirror at the face I had finally gotten to know after winning the high school beauty contest. It was a nice face. I combed my hair back and pinned it into a neat French roll. Back in my bedroom, I slipped on my beige sweater and tan skirt, and then I applied a little lipstick and a pair of small gold hoop earrings. I slipped on my watch—just two pieces of jewelry. The emphasis should be on me, not the jewelry. When I was finished, I walked into the kitchen and asked my mother to wish me luck. "You don't need luck. Just do your best. You'll be all right."

I held on to her words as I walked to the subway station. After waiting five minutes, the A train roared in. In less than thirty minutes, I was in Manhattan and walking down Seventh Avenue. As I neared 27th Street, the FIT building rose up like a monolith. I knew behind many of the windows, there were classrooms in which, even on Saturday morning, students were working on some project, loving the freedom of expressing themselves creatively through their craft.

I entered the building's front door, signed in with the door clerk, and took the elevator up to the top floor. I walked up a short flight of stairs to the rooftop, where the audition would take place. Although it was not yet 9:00, models were assembled there to audition for this opportunity to spend their summer in Moscow.

At precisely 9:00, the audition began. Numbers from the signup sheet were called. We were asked to announce our names clearly and loudly. I couldn't believe some stumbled over their own names or spoke so softly someone had to shout, "Speak louder, dear."

When my number was called, I was already standing. My mother had taught me an old trick—if you didn't want to wrinkle your clothes, you dared not sit down. Even on the subway, there were lots of empty seats, but fearing I'd arrive at the audition in a wrinkled skirt, I didn't dare sit down. When my number was called, I stepped up to the starting point. I looked at an eye level dot on the far wall, and when asked, I said my name clearly and distinctly. Once that was done, like the others, I was asked to walk in a straight line across the floor.

The rooftop was large and spacious, and I walked casually, no fancy footwork, no swinging of the hips, arms casually at my sides, head high! I never looked at those standing nearby for fear doing so would make me nervous, so I looked straight ahead. When I reached the far wall, I turned around, making sure the turn was smooth, unhurried, and natural, and I continued my walk back to where I'd started. I had managed to look calm and casual, although inside my stomach felt like butterflies were playing hockey.

When I was done, someone thanked me. I acknowledged the thanks with a smile. I was finished, but I didn't want to stand around. There was no indication I'd be needed again, and I knew an official notice would be sent to those who were chosen. But as I headed toward the exit door, someone rushed up behind me and whispered in my ear, "You're in." She quickly walked away.

I thanked her, stepped through the door, and happily ran down the stairs. *Wow! I'm going to Moscow!* I shouted inwardly so no one could hear. *Moscow!*

Money was tight for my parents back then, and although there was never a time when they weren't working, having disposable income was a challenge. My mother was afraid I wouldn't have enough money for traveling. But I promised her I would be frugal with what she had already given me, plus I'd have the money I made from my part-time job.

Then I explained, "Once we get to Moscow, each model receives a salary, and my salary will be $240 a week!" I believed my mother was impressed. Her daughter had not yet graduated from college but was already making $240 a week! In 1959, that was an impressive sum.

"What will you do with that money?" my mother asked.

"I'll have to pay bills that I'm responsible for, like my hotel bill."

"How much will that be?" my mother asked, always financially prudent. "I've been told about $12 per week."

"Hmm … $12? And what else will you need to spend money on?"

"Well, we are responsible for our meals, plus carfare to and from Sokolniki Park if we choose not to take the chartered bus. Our first fashion show will begin at 2:00 in the afternoon; we might want to spend the morning sightseeing or sleeping late or having a late breakfast."

"I see," my mother said.

"But guess what, Mom? Every other weekend, a few of us at a time, will be given two days off, and together, we can take the train to visit cities outside of Moscow." My mother looked impressed, and I continued, "Cities like Leningrad and Kiev or religious communities like Zagorsk. Plus, Moscow has a great circus, and they have dozens of concert halls and famous museums! Our salary would allow us to take advantage of Moscow's culture scene and explore other communities."

My mother was relieved, and I saw signs of worry leave her pretty face. For that, I was grateful. Since the time I was a small child, I never wanted to cause her worry or concern.

Fashion Institute of Technology graduation photo

CHAPTER 6

Lady Journalist Pan Show

In two weeks, our group of fifty—forty-seven models and three administrators—would be leaving New York for Moscow. The models ranged in age from four-year-old twins to an attractive silver-haired couple in their sixties. Joe Layton, our choreographer, had rehearsed our group so often we could basically walk the show in our sleep. It was a good feeling to know that if we had to, we could land in Moscow, go directly onto the stage in Sokolniki Park, and do a complete show without missing a beat. So when we were told that Leonard Hankin, the producer of our show, and the president of the retail store, Bergdorph Goodman on West 57th Street and Fifth Avenue in New York City and Eleanor Lambert, a veteran Fashion Industry Publicist who selected the female wardrobe for our fashion show had arranged for us to give a preview performance to 240 lady journalists, we were excited to finally strut our stuff before a real live audience.

The auditorium of the Fashion Institute of Technology played host to the 240 lady journalists. Lights went up, the music started on cue, and our commentator, Vera Bacall, stepped out. Vera Bacall was reportedly related to actress Lauren Bacall, the wife of the late Humphrey Bogart. Vera spoke fluent Russian and would comment on the fashions in Russian to our audiences in Moscow, but tonight she would naturally speak in English for our audience of journalists.

We models entered the stage through one of six revolving doors.

I made my first entrance in a smart off-white light wool dress by American designer Anne Fogarthy. The dress was quite stylish with a little Peter Pan collar, buttons down the front, and long sleeves with French cuffs. It had a few gathers at the waist and seam pockets on each side. My accessories were a brown and white cowhide leather belt that completed the look, with my shoes and handbag matching accordingly. The music cue began, and it was time for me to change for the next scene. Barely one minute later, I was back on stage for the beach scene. It was a quick change because under the wool dress I wore a yellow calico one-piece bathing suit. The wardrobe assistant quickly helped me out of my dress, and placed around my waist the bathing suit's matching calico button-front skirt made to double as a beach cape. Removing my high-heeled shoes I now wore sandals. As I re-entered the stage I had gone from office wear to beachwear in less than a minute!

My favorite scene was the basic black scene. Picture six female models all dressed in plain unadorned basic black dresses, the kind of dress hanging in every women's closet. Smartly dressed male models enter, carrying large hat boxes. Each box contained accessories to spruce up the dresses worn by the models. Inside the boxes were belts, gloves, handbags, necklaces, scarves, and hats to dress up those little black dresses.

Standing in front of the audience, each model added accessories to her little black dress. A belt was added, earrings, a scarf, a hat, perhaps gloves, and a handbag.

As the Russian audience looked on, we believed they would see the versatility of the little black dress and know what to do to spruce up the black dresses they owned. This was the one dress that had the possibility for ten different looks. We believed Russian women would love this scene!

Our wardrobe was snappy and smart, and we completed the entire show in less than forty-five minutes. At the end of the show, we were congratulated by Leonard Hankin, Eleanor Lambert, and Joe Layton for having given performances they were proud of.

But the next morning, newspapers carried a front-page story that spoke of how the ladies of the press hated the show! We wondered what was there to hate. Some of the ladies said they disliked the show's format. They would have liked a more conventional show where the models simply paraded down the runway instead of the scenes with action, music, and dialogue!

One press lady said, "All those people cavorting around on stage and saying, 'Hi!' What are we, a nation of nitwits?" Another said her overall impression of our clothes was "plaid!" The fashion show had an integrated rock 'n roll party scene that they said presented a false picture of American life. They objected to the bridal scene because the bride and groom were white and had an African American best man and maid of honor; it couldn't happen in America, they said. An outdoor picnic was integrated and therefore not representative of American life.

We read what the 240 journalists had said and feared the entire show would be changed to please them. But then blessed telegrams arrived from Leonard Hankin, who assured us we were wonderful. He said he might make some minor changes, but all in all, his vision for the show would remain the same.

He was as good as his word. One of his minor changes was removing me from the rock 'n roll scene, but to tell you the truth, I never felt I was the right type for that scene anyway. I felt I was a sophisticated type and not in a rock 'n roll type.

I believe the wedding with the African American bride and groom who were accompanied by white attendants was also removed. Everything else remained the same. All of the performers breathed a sigh of relief and looked forward to our departure.

U. S. Show Marked by Wide Variety

By GLORIA EMERSON

THE "most sophisticated fashion audience in the world" applauded and cheered yesterday at a preview of the American fashion show to be presented in Moscow.

The audience, which was so described by the executive director of the Fashion Industries Presentation, Leonard J. Hankin, assembled in the auditorium of the Fashion Institute of Technology.

The preview was sponsored by the Pellon Corporation as the opening event of the national Fashion Press Week in New York attended by more than 250 fashion editors from all over the country.

The fashion show, with forty-seven American models, is intended to show an estimated total of 4,000,000 Russians how America dresses. Fashions range from a cotton housedress, priced at about $3 to a Russian sable coat valued at $60,000.

Written and produced by Bert Shevelove, television and trade show producer, and narrated in Russian by Vera Bacal, the show was staged on a copy of the 75-foot-long V-shaped runway to be used in Moscow daily. The show, to be held in Sokolniki Park, as part of the American National Exposition, will run from July 25 to Sept. 5.

In the first scene, models wear costumes representing their own lives. The models include a Princeton undergraduate, a registered nurse, an office worker, a pre-law student, a dancer from "Flower Drum Song" and an actor.

Each scene is staged with vigor, humor and easy-going charm. The models emerge through white doors and occasionally call out a Russian word or two.

The second scene concentrates on play clothes, including bathing suits, camping clothes, ski outfits and golf attire.

In the next scene, which shows civil, church and garden weddings, two of the models, Norma Jean Johnston of New York and Gilbert Noble, are engaged to be married.

One of the most imaginative scenes shows ten similar "little black dresses" ranging from $29 to $395 and carry the message that good taste is not a matter of money in the United States. The ten women who wear them show how they can be changed in a twinkling: male models rush out on the runway with boxes full of handbags, hats, jewelry, belts, gloves and scarves.

Other scenes show clothes by America's most esteemed designers, costumes for travel and picnics and how teen-agers dress and dance to rock 'n' roll music.

The finale is a square dance scene showing cool cottons and country clothes.

Photographed by George Brown for The New York Times

Left: The versatile sheath, costing much or little, is owned by a host of Americans. Jackie Clay wears wool one by Anne Fogarty. $50. Saks 5th, August.
Right: Saluting new state of Alaska, Mary Sinclair, actress, wears Eskimo parka of black and white rabbit fur with gray fox hood. Gray stretch ski pants.

Reprint of New York Times article about Moscow fashion show

CHAPTER 7

Leaving LaGuardia

We were given the opportunity to attend classes to learn to speak a few Russian phrases. It is an interesting language with an alphabet that has thirty-three characters to our twenty-six, so there were a few new sounds for our ears and tongues to adjust to. The tutor helped everyone learn much-needed greetings, salutations, etc. It was fun, and I know we were better for it. If we were talking in our hotel rooms, we were warned to never mention the names of any Russians we'd befriended. Microphones hidden in light bulbs, ceiling fans, or telephones might pick up our conversations. We would never want to give the Secret Police or KGB any traceable information that might lead to a Russian we'd met.

It was also strongly suggested that as we traveled around Moscow, we should carry shiny copper Lincoln pennies with us. Russian children had a fondness for American copper pennies.

It seems that no one in our group had major concerns about going to Russia, even though America and Russia were still in the middle of the Cold War. We felt that if a confrontation had not happened during the past ten years, perhaps both countries might hold off until we returned from what I considered our Good Will Tour. I believe members of our group thought of the war as a very distant thing.

We probably all felt neither country wanted a war, knowing the devastation would be huge. The war had been on hold for a decade; surely it would hold off for another two months! Would we be proven wrong? We certainly hoped not!

In the United States, the average citizen was distrustful of Russia. Communism was a word that caused fear, and those who were suspected of being sympathizers were rooted out. Careers and whole lives were destroyed because of the shadow cast when the word *communism* darkened someone's horizon. It was like there was a putrid scent connected to the word, and Americans crossed to the other side of the street rather than be tainted by it.

To most Americans, our group was considered brave to be going to Russia, a country they only knew as a distant land through the lenses of Hollywood movies. Russia was a country that stood mysteriously hidden behind an Iron Curtain. Even the name "Iron Curtain" presented an image of something cold, impenetrable, and unyielding. So our group of fifty hoped to pierce that curtain—to push it aside to shed some light on the underbelly of Russia, where the tender souls of its people lay, and present the American National Exhibition in Moscow as a delectable slice of American life.

You can perhaps imagine the amount of luggage our group carried. You know how people overpack for a two-week vacation? Imagine packing for a seven-week stay! One case alone was for aspirin, hair preparations, lotions, deodorants, eye drops, cough drops, nail polish, makeup, Band-Aids, and toothpaste—things we weren't sure we'd find in Moscow.

Women in Russia didn't wear makeup; the Communist Party thought such things were frivolous and nonessential. Maybe they were—but we Americans were accustomed to cosmetics and such, so we brought our supply. We weren't sure where we might find feminine products or if such items were available at all.

Unfortunately, we left behind something Americans take for granted. We knew Russia was a country that didn't pamper its citizens or go out of its way to provide creature comforts. Something as simple as toilet paper was not a product to be found anywhere because it was not a top-priority item in Russia at that time. You would make do with strips of newspaper tacked to the inside of your bathroom stall. Crumble the newspaper up to soften it a bit, and then brace yourself for its scratchiness.

In some upper-crust establishments, we found little squares of paper—perhaps five by five inches and with the consistency of wax paper. We

Americans delighted in it because it made excellent writing paper with a look of parchment paper. But if it was used for its intended purpose, it too had to be crumbled and softened before use.

It took twelve hours for us to fly out of LaGuardia Airport on July 19, 1959! We were scheduled to depart at 11:00 a.m., so naturally, we arrived at the airport early. Our group was a group of fifty, and we wanted no snafus with passports, immunizations papers, or whatever else might cause a delay. Of course, each model was accompanied by parents, family, and friends who wanted to see us off and wish us well on such an unprecedented journey.

Our flight was to leave from La Guardia's Terminal D, and with family and friends in tow, we arrived ready to board our plane. Once we were at Terminal D, we turned to those who had gotten up early to see us off, exchanged hugs and kisses, and told them how much they were appreciated. Some goodbyes came with tear-filled eyes, but before they could leave, we were told there had been a change in our flight plans. We were instructed to go to Terminal B, where we would catch a slightly later flight. Looking at our guests sheepishly and knowing this wasn't going to be goodbye, with good humor, we all trudged through the airport to Terminal B.

When we arrived slightly winded at Terminal B, we learned that Terminal A had been selected for our departure, and we were to get over there posthaste! On the double, we rushed through the airport—mothers, fathers, aunts, uncles, grandmothers and grandpas, brothers and sisters, neighbors and friends with babies in strollers—to get to Terminal A in a timely fashion. Surely after fruitless trips to three different terminals that seemed miles apart, there wouldn't be another change, but of course there was! This pilgrimage was no longer cute.

Our core group was fifty in number, but when you added friends and family members there to see us off, we became a group of nearly two hundred moving en masse through LaGuardia Airport. We were a caravan, moving from terminal to terminal, hopeful that the next announcement might ensure a stop to this seemingly aimless roaming. But again, as we gnashed our teeth, we were informed the flight time had changed, and we would now leave later and from yet another terminal!

I became concerned about the older members of our entourage, but they were made of tough stuff and gamely kept up with our pilgrimage. The children were kept placated with food stuffs like hot dogs, jelly-filled donuts, and dripping ice cream. Certainly no one complained, but this migration had long ago lost its appeal.

Finally we got the okay that our flight would definitely leave by 8:00 p.m. Most of us had arrived at the airport at 8:00 that morning. The journey through LaGuardia had lasted twelve hours! Plus, we'd said goodbye so many times that those goodbyes became meaningless and passé!

Instead of an emotional send off, it was coming down to a slap on the back and a "See ya when you get back!" Of course no one would admit it, but those who had come to see us off would be happy to see us go!

Wearily, we arrived at Terminal C, and an actual plane was waiting. Perhaps a waiting plane was a good sign. We heard the words we had been longing to hear since early that morning: "You may board." With good humor, we turned to those who had been with us for twelve long hours, and again we hugged and kissed each other goodbye.

We boarded the plane, and maybe it was exhaustion, but we felt less like fashion models and more like soldiers suffering battle fatigue. Seats were not assigned, so I took one by a window. Warren Lyons, son of *New York Post* feature writer Leonard Lyons, famous for his column, "In The Lyons Den," and Warren's brother, Jeffery Lyons, the movie critic, stood smiling down at me. "I want to sit next to you," Warren said, looking over at me, "because I've heard women of color are beautiful when they wake up in the morning!"

I had to laugh, and then I thought whoever was spreading that rumor was okay with me. I welcomed Warren to the seat next to me. I wasn't going to debate with him on that rumor because I kind of liked it.

Warren placed his bags in the overhead, sat down, and strapped himself in. When all was secure and the doors were finally closed, our plane taxied down the runway, and soon we were in a position to take off. We all peered out our windows to take one last look at New York City's skyline. Exhaustion settled in, and in less than fifteen minutes, almost everyone on board was sound asleep!

It felt like only minutes, but it must have been a few hours when we landed to refuel in Goose Bay, Canada. We got out of the plane and walked carefully across the packed ice to their station. While the plane was refueled, we drank hot chocolate and had snacks. Then we boarded our plane, and the journey continued.

Our next refueling stop was in Ireland. We were impressed with Ireland's beautiful Shannon River. Streaks of sunlight sent silvery shimmers over the surface of its tranquil waters. Ireland appeared serene now. The all-too-real stories of Irishmen of the Catholic faith at war with Irishmen of the Protestant faith seemed nonexistent now. All was calm and peaceful as we made our way to the Shannon Airport Gift Shop.

On display was the silver jewelry skillfully made by local Irish craftsmen. I spotted a sterling silver marquisette ring. I thought my mother would like it, and the price fit my budget. I could almost hear her saying, "Save your money," but I bought it and tucked it away to give to her when I returned home.

Back on the plane, we were told our next refueling stop would be Stockholm, so we got comfortable in our seats and slept a few more hours. We would be in Stockholm several hours, so Mrs. Goodman arranged a bus tour of the city.

As the bus wove its way through Stockholm, we noted that the city was quaint and lively with colorful lights, busy eating places, movie theaters, fresh food stands, and lots of clothing stores. "Notice anything unusual?" someone on our bus spoke out.

"Does it have anything to do with the women?" another person asked.

"Wow! Look at the women!" someone said when they finally noticed a strange trend among the ladies of Stockholm. We focused on the women, and suddenly, everyone saw it!

"I thought I was seeing things!" the girl behind me said. "Amazing. All the women—and I mean *all* the women—have dyed their hair blond, and the exact same shade of blond!"

"And all are wearing their hair in precisely the same style!" someone else pointed out.

"I bet I know who they're imitating," a voice from the rear of the bus shouted.

"Yep, I know too!" came back a reply. "They are all trying to look like ..."

"Yep! Can you believe the impact this movie star has made?"

"Hey, it's that French movie star they're all trying to look like; what's her name?"

"Oh, I know who," a male voice blurted out. "It's ... it's ... oh, heck ... what's her name ... I got it, it's Bridget Bardot!"

"Oh, yeah!" we all shouted. "Bridget Bardot!"

Whether the Stockholm women were tall or short; young or middle-aged, shopping, biking, or pushing a baby in a stroller, all were replicas of Bridget Bardot.

After our bus tour was complete, we again boarded our plane. We were now on the final leg of our journey. As our plane sliced through the placid night skies, we were told that in a few hours, we would touch down in Moscow.

The pilot skillfully landed in Vnukovo Airport in Moscow. There was an eleven-hour time difference between Moscow and New York, so it was about 4:30 a.m. in Moscow and dark. We gathered our things together to exit the plane we had flown in for the last twenty-four hours. We gathered our carry-on bags, lined up to exit the plane, and when we filed out the door, our passports—which had been collected in New York—were returned to us.

Silently, we disembarked, too excited to talk, trying to stay focused on what the airport procedures might be. Out on the tarmac, we breathed in the air of Moscow. *Our first intake of Moscow air. Silly,* I thought. *Stay focused.*

Looking around and standing against the darkened building were Russian men dressed in what looked like work clothes, motionless in the shadows. We were unable to see individual faces, just silhouettes and eyes that darted about, watching us. I wondered who they were and thought their formation, lined up against the terminal wall in the dark, was odd. We all felt a little uneasy about those men but continued our walk in the chilly predawn air. All the while, those silent men remained standing in the shadows, watching. We watched them too until we entered the terminal.

Glancing back, we saw that the men were still standing as before but had found something else of interest to watch. I labeled them "the watchers." They were probably harmless, just constantly monitoring on their own time who was coming and going at the airport.

Safely inside the terminal, we inquired where we might find our luggage. The reply was vague, as we were told our luggage was inside one of the rooms. No specific room was given, so we checked each room we passed until we found our luggage. Haphazardly piled one on top of the other, our bags formed a stack high enough to almost touch the ceiling of this enormous room. We stood back and studied the pile, trying to decide how to tackle the job of securing individual bags. But the answer was piece by piece, one suitcase at a time. Each model had at least two suitcases containing enough clothes to get us through the next seven weeks.

There were also many trunks containing the wardrobe for the fashion show. Six hundred garments and accessories were packed in huge trunks. There was no help from the airport personnel, so we were on our own. It was a slow, tedious process that literally took hours. Piece by piece, we reduced the massive pile.

Each piece of luggage was loaded onto our waiting chartered bus outside. At last, we were able to emerge from the airport and board the bus that would take us to our hotel.

Chapter 8

Sunrise in Moscow

Exhausted, we dragged our bodies onto the chartered bus, hardly able to keep our eyes open. We looked forward to arriving at our hotel and taking a shower, a nap, and then a good dinner in the hotel dining room. But as our bus left the airport, the sun began to rise over the city of Moscow, and of course, we were wide awake again! "Look," Warren said while pointing up. I looked up and was surprised to see a huge full-color poster of the movie, *War and Peace.* And there were Audrey Hepburn and Mel Ferrer. We were all surprised to see an American film playing at a theater in Moscow!

Now the sun was fully up and waking up the city of Moscow. Ordinary things interested us, like seeing Russians who were on their way to work. Several stood reading the morning newspaper as they held coffee in paper cups and waited for their bus to arrive. When you only see Russian leaders in the newspapers, you forget about the ordinary people, the common Russian, the man hoping the bus won't be late in getting him to work on time.

Perhaps an hour later, our chartered bus pulled up in front of the Hotel Ostankino. We were relieved to finally come to the end of our six thousand mile journey.

I think we expected an exotic hotel, but the Ostankino looked like an austere office building. There were no trees gracefully lining a walkway nor beds of colorful flowers or green plants adorning a cobblestone path. There was only concrete all around. But after traveling for twenty-four hours, we were happy they could provide us with a room, bed, shower, and place where we would then put on a fresh change of clothes.

The hotel staff seemed overwhelmed with fifty people checking in all at once, but they carried out their duties efficiently. The inside of the hotel looked similar to the outside. The interior was drab like a dusty nursing home. Nondescript paint covered the walls. Were the walls painted a brown or gray, or were they a mixture of both? The carpet on the floor was reflective of the walls. Nothing shined or sparkled. Everything had the look of having been placed there years ago, and no one had since done anything to spruce it up.

With room keys in hand, we took the lift, a charming relic from yesteryear, up to our rooms. The lift is a cage-like box, usually made of a fancy wrought iron design through which the rider can see each floor as it is passed. The lift, our elevator, was pulled by exposed cables that slowly took us to the upper floors and back down again when needed.

After exiting the lift and taking a short walk down the hall, we found our rooms. But we were shocked when we realized the rooms had no bathrooms. When called to inquire, the hotel representative did not speak English well. We in our quickie Russian languish course in New York had not learned the Russian words for "Why is there no bathroom in my room?" But we were told we'd find the bathroom located down the hall.

Ah, she was right—there was a bathroom down the hall. But the bathroom accommodated one person at a time. We got back on the phone with the hotel representative again, and on a happy note, we were told there was an identical bathroom located on the floor below! What more could you want? So all forty-seven of us had the option of using either one of two bathrooms!

The situation was what it was! We decided among just our group to begin a number system and set a required length of time for each bathroom stay. No one could stay in the bathroom longer than ten to fifteen minutes. It was agreed. We used the bathrooms in shifts and managed to get through that first day. Our next issue was also a major concern. It was late July, and it was a delightful eighty degrees in Moscow. But as we sat in our room, discussing the bathroom situation, the room began feeling stuffy and hot.

We tried to solve this problem by ourselves by looking for the cooling system. When we found it, it wasn't working, so we called the front desk to ask for someone to come and fix it.

A young Russian maintenance man came up to check it out. He tinkered with the device for about ten minutes but had no luck in locating the problem. In short order, he packed up his tools and offered no apologies as he left and indicated we should open the windows if we wanted ventilation. But we took his advice, slid the windows open, and discovered the screens were torn. Ah, fresh air—but the repair guy was right; we had ventilation. Unfortunately, because of the torn screens, mosquitoes, flies, and other insects found their way in. Russian mosquitoes had the same nasty habits of biting as American mosquitoes, so we had to make peace with that situation as well. We took turns using the bathrooms, but of course, no dawdling was allowed. After we showered, we laid down for a short nap. When we awoke a few hours later, we were ready to visit the hotel's dining room and have our very first meal in Moscow.

The restaurant was located on the first floor, and the waiters approached our table with menus. We rejoiced because the menus had pictures of the food they served. Pictures of the food was a cool idea. When the waitress came to take our orders, we gave her the number on the pictured item.

Off she went while we waited. We noticed that the dining room was very busy with people from various countries, and we talked amongst ourselves as we waited. Soon an hour had passed, but we decide we'd give them a few more minutes.

Finally, realizing how much time had elapsed, we flagged down our waitress. We repeated the order we had placed but worried plenty when we saw a vacant look in her eyes. Her look said one or two things—she didn't recognize us as having placed an order, or she thought our order had been delivered. In trying to figure out what had happened to our order, it seemed the order was either never turned in or our food had been delivered to another table. We had to reorder.

To visit the hotel dining room from that day on was always an experience. I was told the waiters worked twenty-four-hour shifts, so by the time we perky Americans came down, the waiters were totally spent! Mishaps were common, and service was too slow, so we realized that if we were really hungry, we'd eat elsewhere!

Also staying at Hotel Ostankino was a large delegation of Chairman Mao's Red Chinese or Communist Chinese men who were celebrating an obviously important private event. The Chinese men stayed to themselves, never speaking to anyone outside of those in their group. They never smiled, and I felt those muscles needed for smiling had never been used. As a matter of fact, their speaking voices were never heard as they talked in hushed tones. If two or three were talking together in the hotel lobby and a guest walked by, their conversation stopped immediately. When that guest was out of hearing range, their conversation continued. I think they feared some hotel guest had a working knowledge of Cantonese or Mandarin. From the American group, I could assure them we had enough as we struggled to speak Russian!

The temperature was consistently in the eighties. So naturally, it seemed odd that the Communist Chinese men wore high-collared, long-sleeved wool military suits.

One evening, thirty men assembled for a private celebration in the Ostankino's large conference room. They had eaten their dinner on a sturdy, dark wooden table. When finished, waiters quickly removed all plates and utensils, leaving only drinking glasses in front of each man, sitting on both sides of the long table. A door suddenly opened, and a young Chinese girl of five or six was escorted into the room. As she walked, I at first only noticed her knee length red satin dress and black shoes. But when she was lifted to stand on the table, I noticed her shiny black hair, pearl-like skin, and intelligent, watchful eyes. Cleared of utensils and dishes, there was now a clear path down the center of the long table. Music sounded, and the girl began a song that I was told was in tribute to the military men in the room. Then she danced skillfully down the length of the table. She was precision itself. She never overturned a single glass! She spun, turned, and sang with conviction. Stone-faced, the men watched as the child covered the distance from one end of the table to the other. Her red dress flashed past the seated men as she continued singing the song in praise of their loyalty to their homeland. At the end, the music stopped, the men clapped, and the doll-like dancer took a quick bow. She stood on the table breathing heavily. Like the men her face showed no emotion. Finally, a pair of hands lifted her off the table and quickly escorted her across the room and out the door.

The soldiers remained seated, some quietly talking while perhaps letting the child's flawless performance resonate. Eventually, one by one, the military men rose from their chairs and cleared the room.

One morning, I waited in the dining room for my coffee, a blinsky (a pancake rolled and stuffed with jelly and cooked beef), and scrambled eggs. I had come extra early to order breakfast, having experienced how slow the service was. While waiting, I remembered some post cards I left in my room and had planned to mail that day. Knowing how slow the service was, I knew I could return to my room, get the post cards, and mail them all before breakfast was delivered. So I quickly left my table, proceeded out the dining room, and went into the lobby to take the lift. I looked up and noticed three Chinese men standing near the elevator.

On previous days, I certainly found their behavior intimidating and realized I was uncomfortable even with the thought of passing by them. I stopped and stood in the middle of the lobby, not wanting to take another step in their direction. But I soon felt my own behavior was childish. Why was I avoiding them just because their behavior was different from what I was familiar with? I asked myself why I was so intimidated. They had never done anything to me. I now felt ashamed of my own behavior as I stood undecided as to whether to return to the dining room or go for it, charge past them, and ring for the elevator.

Silly me, I chided myself, *you're in a hotel, for goodness sake. Grow up!* Slowly harnessing my courage, I proceeded across the lobby, mounted the steps, and as I drew closer, as expected, they immediately stopped talking and stood silently facing each other. I didn't look their way and quickly mounted the three steps and prepared to ring for the lift. As my hand was in midair, you can't imagine my surprise when one of the Chinese men said, in perfect English, "Hi, babe!"

Shocked, I stood still, facing the lift that was slowly descending. I wondered where the man had heard that phrase. Could credit be given to Hollywood, as the man who spoke might have seen some Hollywood movies where "Hi, babe" had been spoken? What was I to do? After all, one of them had spoken to me, so should I not return the greeting?

With my decision made, I spun around, wanting to say "Hi" to whomever had spoken to me. But as I turned, I was met with blank expressions. I looked at the two who were facing me, but their eyes looked off into the distance, and the third man who had his back to me never turned around. Which of the three had spoken? Slowly, I turned and entered the lift. The gated doors clamored shut, and I looked at the men as the lift rose, taking me up to my floor. But I smiled as I realized that "Hi, babe" had been a significant moment. Verbally, one man had ventured out to greet me. In that greeting, I felt there was a victory of sorts!

CHAPTER 9

Russian Experiences

During our first week in Moscow, we were invited to a celebration at the Sudanese Consulate in Moscow. It was a black tie affair. I was excited about getting out and seeing what being in Moscow had to offer. The Consulate was located in a stately brick building on a quiet street. The Sudanese men were very impressive-looking, dark brown-skinned people whom I had never seen before, and they impressed me! Most wore uniforms decorated with medals. I knew those medals denoted their ranks in the Sudanese Army.

I didn't see them mingling with the guests and felt them to be slightly aloof, but their keen facial features and dark wavy hair made them appear quite handsome to me. If there were any Sudanese women there that night, I did not see them. But the men carried themselves in a proud military manner.

We were assembled in a large white dining room. Besides the dance floor, there were at least ten rectangular tables with white cotton table cloths, and each of us sat before a pretty table setting consisting of a gleaming china dinner plate and utensils. Above each plate sat an empty six ounce crystal glass. I wondered if the waiter would fill the glasses with juice or tea.

To my surprise, when the waiter did come around, he filled each glass with pure Russian vodka, a drink I'd never had before. *It looks harmless,* I thought of the vodka that looked as clear as drinking water.

I believe what happened next was a Russian custom, but one by one, each guest stood, held his or her glass high in a toast, and while everyone watched, that individual drank all the vodka in his or her glass without stopping. I watched each swallow of vodka go down. Even though I'd never tasted vodka before, how difficult could it be to swallow a liquid that looked like water?

I wondered if this was some kind of endurance test, but when my turn came, I stood, extended the arm that held my glass, and said "Prost." Then I returned the glass to my lips and drank until my glass was drained. The vodka went down smoothly, and the taste was unlike anything I had ever tasted before. I tried to decide if I liked it while I sat waiting to feel its effect, but at that moment, I felt nothing unusual.

A big guy who was either Russian or German came over to ask me to dance. "Do you speak Dutch?" he asked as we danced.

I remembered answering, "No, I don't speak German." I laughed, wondering if I had said what I meant or was the vodka speaking. Suddenly, I felt tipsy and wanted to go to bed.

I decided from that night on that vodka and I would go our separate ways. For the remainder of my stay in Russia, vodka was not my beverage of choice.

One night, as a few of the models and I talked, I mentioned that I had never had a birthday party. Oh, my birthday was celebrated, but not by having a party. It did not seem unusual to me, but my friends thought such a thing was highly unusual and should be rectified immediately! They decided we'd have a party in our hotel room. If I could find a shop in Moscow where I could buy a few balloons, they might add a little color to the drab decor. The other models volunteered to bring caviar, crackers, soda, vodka, and cookies. Russian ice cream was delicious, so someone would buy it for the party. But my contribution was to be ten colorful balloons.

That Wednesday, when the last fashion show of the day ended, I dressed quickly because I discovered there was a shop across the street from Sokolniki Park that sold balloons, and the staff would blow them up and attach strings to each. I watched as each balloon expanded into a pretty orb of gay colors. The clerk gave me each one until I had a total of ten. The balloons bobbed and weaved and reminded me of frisky puppies on a leach. I paid the lady, thanked her, and left the shop.

It was the end of July, and the weather in Moscow was again perfect. Watching the traffic, I made my way across the street and to the corner, where I promised to wait for my roommate, Linda. I stood off to the side so that people could pass and my balloons and I wouldn't be in the way.

I was wearing a light cotton summer dress, and the skirt of my dress billowed in the gentle breeze. I held on tightly to my buoyant balloons, as they seemed to dance on their strings—happy, I assumed, to have been rescued from the balloon box in the shop.

People walked by, but I never gave much thought to how a black girl standing on a street corner in Moscow holding a bunch of balloons might look to Russians passing by. What did they think as they looked at me? As they sat around the dinner table, what would they say about seeing some black girl standing on the corner, holding balloons?

Again, I tried looking down the street to see if Linda was coming. I realized the once moving pedestrians were no longer moving but had stopped and had silently and literarily surrounded me. I was pinned in. Taken aback, I looked at the faces of those Russians who stood closest to me, and they stared back, their eyes cold and unblinking. I knew I was a curiosity, but I didn't expect Russians to interrupt their trips home to stop and stare. To say I felt uneasy, being surrounded by this crowd who stared unsmiling at me, would be an understatement. But the last thing I wanted was to appear afraid. So I looked up at my balloons, thankful for them because they gave me something to focus on.

Perhaps I could command the balloons to lift me up above the heads of these unfriendly-looking people. Of course, I knew such an escape was not possible. I was on my own, unable to fathom why these Russians found me of interest, especially in what I sensed was a hostile way. I wondered if perhaps the crowd saw me as a threat of some kind, but then, how dangerous could a girl in a cotton dress be, with her only arsenal being ten bobbing balloons?

Finally, I looked down at a tattered little Russian boy who stood as part of this crowd. The child was barefoot, and the clothes he had on were unfortunately dirty, threadbare, and raggedy. He was the kind of Russian child you never saw on the streets in Moscow. No, children like this were kept out of sight.

Although I had seen poor Russian children like this little boy on Lenin Hill, a hill that was the highest point in Moscow and was located on the left bank of the Moskva River, the Russian government wanted the look of a perfect society. Drunkenness, handicapped people, and anyone showing signs of poverty were kept out of sight. The government wanted the city of Moscow to appear picture-perfect. Visitors were to leave with the impression that all Russians were perfect in body and mind.

As I stood surrounded by these stone-faced Russians, I remembered I had several Lincoln copper pennies in my small handbag. Before we left New York, we had been advised to always carry them. I had not needed to use them before, so I hoped they would work some magic now. "Would you like one?" I asked the boy as I extended my hand toward him, holding one of those shiny Lincoln pennies.

In what seemed to be a Russian custom, children never accepted a gift if they didn't have one to offer in return. So the boy took the penny but handed me a pin of Lenin. It was a silent exchange, but I took his gift, smiled, and thanked him in Russian.

To my astonishment, a woman, perhaps in her late forties or early fifties, spoke to me in perfect English. "You like children?" she asked. Her voice was stern and her eyes hard as they stared at me, almost challenging me—but to what I didn't know.

I looked at her, ignoring the others who stood silently observing. "Yes," I answered truthfully, "I like children."

With that, she followed her first question with another that was equally as puzzling to me. "You like *Russian* children?" Surely that wasn't an accusation. If so, what was the basis for it? Had their propaganda said Americans did not like Russian children?

I was at a loss as to where this line of questioning was coming from. But again, I looked this woman in the eye and spoke with surety so that my answer could not be interpreted as anything but the truth. "Yes, I like *all* children!" I said firmly.

My response must have satisfied her, because the crowd, as though on cue, dispersed and silently drifted away.

I was again standing alone as before, but this time they left me much to think about. I remembered reading that back in the 1930s, when Stalin was on a quest to erase religion from Russia, he was instrumental in starting propaganda lies that the Baptists in the Russian church were not Baptists but American spies. Then Stalin went on to compound the lies by adding these American spies ate Russian children!

Is that why the Russian woman in the crowd asked specifically if I liked Russian children? Was she, all these years later, the victim of Stalin's propaganda? I was on the verge of walking away when Linda finally showed up. "Hi, were you thinking of leaving?" she asked.

"How did you guess?"

"Well, I thought you might have gotten bored waiting."

I looked up at my balloons, neglecting to mention my encounter with the Russian crowd. It would have been too complicated to explain. "Oh, believe me," I said, "I was far from bored." And I smiled to myself as Linda and I and my balloons mingled with the Russian crowd.

For nearly two weeks, our group had put up with the limitations that existed at the Ostankino hotel. Many had begun calling the Ostankino "Old Stinko!" But luckily, with the guidance of the gracious Mrs. Shirley Goodman, we were moving to the Leningradskya Hotel. The Leningradskya was a fabulous hotel from a grand era located in the heart of Moscow. The Kremlin and Red Square were nearby. All city buses stopped at the Leningradskya as well as taxicabs.

Plus, every room had a bathroom of its own.

CHAPTER 10

The Stranger on the Bus

Spying was not a new occupation, but during the Cold War, spying flourished. The most notorious of modern-day spies were the Cambridge Four, and they became legendary. Recruited while still students at Cambridge University, they were clever and charismatic, which allowed them to move freely between British Parliament and the White House. Publicly, they professed a disdain for Communism and a loyalty for their homeland and her allies. These were all lies!

Recruited in 1945, most of the Cambridge Four were still operating undetected fifty years later. Through the years, these men—Philby, Maclean, Brunt, and Burgess—caused the deaths of thousands as they fed damaging information about England and America to the KGB. They were never apprehended, each living out the remainder of their lives in Russia. Kim Philby, who served the KGB for fifty years and was dubbed "The Spy of the Century," died in Russia in 1988.

Nevertheless, visiting Moscow in 1959, one should have been aware of the garden-variety spies who were alive and well and operating locally. During this era, it was common for neighbor to spy against neighbor, wives to spy against husbands, and the reverse for whatever brownie points the

KGB metered out. Summer in Moscow was definitely not an innocent affair like April in Paris, so stranger beware.

I had been in Russia slightly longer than two weeks when I had an encounter with the stranger on the bus. It all began innocently enough with my accepting an invitation to see a Russian puppet show.

Jason was a young African American, born with a passion for languages. As a student in New York City, he studied Russian and became so fluent in it that he landed a job as a tour guide at the American National Exhibition in Moscow. But Jason had another passion, and to my surprise, it was puppetry! He had researched the various forms of puppetry and was convinced the Russians excelled in this art form. He felt sure if I saw one Russian puppet show, I too would be convinced that in puppetry, the Russians were the best on the planet. So I accepted his invitation to a nearby theater to see an actual Russian puppet show.

Usually a taxi would be our mode of transportation, but after being in Moscow nearly two weeks, neither Jason nor I had ridden on a city bus. So we took the bus to the theater and were there in less than twenty minutes. Inside the theater, puppetry enthusiasts filled every seat. Just as the house lights began to dim, we found our seats, and seconds later, the lights came up on the stage and the puppets sprang to life. They looked like life-sized dolls, only these dolls were amazingly animated as the puppeteers gave movement to their heads, arms, and legs, making them stomp their feet in defiance or dance skillfully across the stage, lighter than air. They were dressed in clothes that were replicas of those worn in some Russian provinces. I watched as the puppets talked, fussed, and romped through their scenes, making the audience laugh with their humorous antics. Jason was my translator, and I found myself laughing along with the crowd of Russians.

When the show ended and the lights came up, the talented puppeteers introduced themselves, and each received a rousing round of applause from the appreciative audience.

Jason and I left the theater and joined those who were already outside waiting in line for the bus to arrive. It was a pleasant evening, about seventy degrees, even though it was nearly 11:00. I looked up at the sky over Moscow, and it was a deep, dark blue sky with brightly twinkling stars and a lovely amber moon. Our bus finally pulled up and opened its back door, and all in line began to board.

We entered the back door of the bus, and there stood a uniformed female attendant to whom we gave one kopek, our bus fare (less than an American penny), which the attendant received without comment.

Jason and I walked down the center aisle, still talking about the funny moments from the puppet show. We found two seats positioned directly behind the bus driver. The bus driver was separated from his passengers by a thick clear plastic wall that placed him in his own private compartment. As a result, he was unable to hear any chatter from his passengers as he drove along his route.

As I looked at people boarding the bus, I found myself taking note of a man making his way down the bus aisle toward us. My first and most immediate impression was that this well-dressed, thirty-something white male wearing an oversized dark wool coat was American. He moved slowly, passing several empty seats, finally ending up standing in front of Jason and me.

In facing us, his back was to the seated passengers behind him. For some reason, I was not curious as to why he was wearing a big coat on such a mild night. The way the stranger was dressed did not seem odd but simply added to his Americanized look.

He stood over us, supporting himself by placing his arms over the overhead bar as his great coat flared out on both sides, creating a kind of cocoon, allowing the three of us to talk privately while shielded from the curious eyes of the bus riders.

As we talked, we looked up into his clear blue eyes, which appeared kind and sincere. His brown hair was cut close and seemed freshly trimmed in a style that neatly framed his attractive face. "Are you American?" was his first question as he gave us a warm and engaging smile.

"Yes." Jason and I responded almost in unison; we were both a little taken aback, being approached by an English-speaking man on a bus in Moscow.

"I was an American, too," the stranger volunteered as his smile faded for a quick moment.

"Was?" I asked in surprise. I had never met a former American.

"Yes," he answered, and he sighed heavily. "I was twenty-one years old and a political science major."

"Where?" Jason asked quickly, almost with a challenge in his voice.

"At the University of Michigan," he said.

"You defected?" Jason asked, making sure he had heard the stranger.

"Oh, yes," the stranger said, captivating us with his direct stare. "I was approached by a man on campus one day who suggested if I were to defect to the Soviet Union, I could have a great political career. I believed him."

Jason and I listened in quiet fascination. "Well, have you had a great career?" I asked, wanting to know if defecting had been worth it.

"That was thirteen years ago!" the stranger admitted, but he added, almost bitterly, "So far, no great career."

We were unable to respond to such an amazing story and one we least expected after a fun night at a puppet show. My mind churned with questions, but it was the stranger who spoke again. "I was a sports fan! Tell me, how are the various teams doing?" The stranger turned to Jason. I had no knowledge of such things, but Jason followed sports, and the two talked on while I wondered about a twenty-one-year-old student who left behind everything and everyone he knew for the promise of a career in a distant land.

"Do you correspond with your family?" I interrupted their sports chatter, insisting on asking about family, which was still very important to me, especially since I was the age he had been when he defected thirteen years ago.

To my surprise, instead of an answer, the stranger reached into his inside coat pocket and pulled out a letter-sized white envelope and handed it to me.

Instinctively, I took it, but I felt immediately uncomfortable holding it. As a result, I barely looked at the name and address, not wanting to appear as though I was prying. But I did notice the envelope was sealed as though ready to be mailed. "My mother has written to tell me she is dying of cancer," the stranger said simply. "In every letter she writes, she begs me to come home."

We listened stupefied as he related another heartbreaking story of his life. "I immediately went to the Russian authorities," he said. "I asked permission to return home to America because my mother might soon die."

Jason and I listened, hardly breathing. It was unbearable for me to think of my own mother dying as his mother was, pleading to see her child one last time. I couldn't speak for Jason, but I was sold, and my heart went out to this stranger. "It's been more than a decade since I last saw my mother," the stranger told us. "In order to go home, I needed an exit visa, but it was denied!"

"Denied?" the word escaped my lips in a shrill sound of disbelief. "How could they deny you the opportunity to see a parent who was dying?"

The stranger only gave a shrug of his shoulders to my startled response. "I have written several letters to my mother," the Stranger continued, "telling her I'm not able to leave Russia. But in her very next letter, she continues to beg me to come home."

Jason and I sat in silence, neither of us knowing how to respond. "I began to think," he continued, "perhaps she wasn't getting my letters." He seemed to be testing his theory on us. "Or were my letters being intercepted? Information perhaps blacked out, making it impossible for her to read why I'm unable to come home!" The stranger looked at us as though we might have answers. We sat mute; any answers to his incredible story were surely unknown to us.

"Is that even possible, that your personal mail could be tampered with?" I asked, knowing how foolish that question was. In my heart, I felt the government in Russia did not hold the individual in high esteem. The individual did not matter to the Russian government.

The bus approached our stop. I was still holding the envelope the stranger had handed to me, but some instinct prompted me to give it back. When I did, he quickly claimed it. I looked to see any signs of regret that I was returning it. Nor were there any whispered suggestions of my keeping the letter to mail once I returned home. Instead, he quickly took the letter from my hand and hastily replaced it in his inside coat pocket. "This is where we get off," I said to the stranger.

He then stepped aside as we left the privacy of our cocoon. "Be careful whom you befriend while you're in Russia," the stranger advised us. We acknowledged his advice. "I'll be leaving for the Republic of Georgia in a few days, so I won't be seeing you again."

We nodded as we inched toward the door, saying goodbye and wishing him a safe trip to Georgia. The bus stopped, and we disembarked.

As the bus pulled off, through the window, we could see the stranger looking out after us. Jason and I stood on the sidewalk, rooted to the spot where the bus had left us. We were conflicted, unable to walk away, perhaps letting that emotional experience wear off.

The envelope I'd returned to him suddenly loomed as a decision I now somehow regretted. "Should I have kept the envelope with the letter the stranger had written to his mother?" I enquired of Jason. "Kept it in my suitcase … mailed it from home? His mother might get it in time … to know why … her son …" I let the words trail off.

"You think so?" Jason asked, looking as perplexed as I felt.

"I mean, to bring her comfort … in the end."

"Yeah," Jason said, sighing, perhaps still not totally convinced.

We glanced up the street, looking after the bus that carried the Stranger. In the dark, we could only see the bus's fading tail lights. I promised myself then that if I ever ran into the stranger again, I would ask him for the letter. I would keep it safe until I was in New York and then mail it.

The plight of the stranger was so upsetting, I said goodnight to Jason, went up to my hotel room, and immediately placed a call to my mother. In the two weeks I'd been in Moscow, I'd made contact, but not by phone. But tonight I wanted to hear my mother's voice. How the stranger had been treated by the government he'd chosen over his own was disturbing to me. I wondered how people made such messes of their lives. It was clear that the stranger had given away his freedoms, and no one could rescue him now.

I entered my room, sat on the bed, and picked up the telephone. I gave the hotel operator my phone number in Brooklyn, New York. After a few seconds of silence, the operator came on the line, telling me there was something wrong with my phone and that she would send a mechanic up to repair it.

Strange, I thought as I listened to her, *it had been working fine.* But I said okay and replaced the receiver. Twenty minutes later, a mechanic knocked and entered my room. I watched as he took the phone apart and then put it back together again. Without hardly a glance at me, he indicated the phone was fixed and left. I dialed the operator again. She checked the number I had given her earlier and instructed me to hang up but stay near the phone so I could answer it when the call came through. I sat and waited, but there was no call. Then I lay on the bed and waited. When my phone was still silent, I took a shower, put on my night gown, lay on my bed, and waited, but when no call came through, I fell asleep.

The next morning, I was feeling better, and speaking to my mother no longer seemed urgent. The stranger had said we wouldn't be seeing him again, so I decided to move on. Any noble gestures I might have imagined that would have helped his mother understand why her son wasn't at her bedside were never in my control anyway.

But two days later, at 1:00 in the morning, someone banged on my door, telling me I had a phone call in her room. "In her room?" I looked at my phone, which sat silently on the night stand. Why would I have a phone call in her room?

Again, there was more banging and a voice telling me I had a phone call. She said I was to come to her room right away.

I jumped out of bed, wondering if it was the call I had placed two nights ago. Had that call finally come through? Had it come through but on someone else's a phone?

I opened my door and stood face-to-face with a young girl. "The operator says you have a call on the phone in my room," she said with a heavy Slavic accent.

"Thank you. Where is your room?" I asked.

"Follow me." And she led me to her room.

We entered, and a man and woman stood looking sleepy and like they wanted to know what was going on.

I said, *"Dobry vyechyer,"* and quickly walked over and picked up the telephone. "Hello," I said.

"Hello," the voice at the other end replied. The voice was so clear, like the speaker was next door. But the voice sounded so near that I doubted this could be my call. I had been awakened from a deep sleep; perhaps my brain was foggy. "Who is this?" I demanded of the person on the other end.

Calmly, my mother said, "It's me. How are you?" I finally recognized her voice.

"I'm fine, Mom." I calmed down. "I just wanted to know how you were doing."

"I'm doing okay, you?" she asked again.

"I'm fine, Mom."

"You sure?" she asked.

"Yes, I'm doing great!"

"All right. Enjoy your day," she said.

"You too, Mom. Bye."

"Bye," I heard her say as the connection ended.

I hung up the phone. "Wow, my mother's voice from six thousand miles away!"

I looked at the occupants of this room as they stood looking at me. They were a family, a man and wife and two teenage daughters. I felt I needed to explain. "I'm so sorry, but the hotel operator made a mistake!" I said, looking at them. "You see, that was my mother ..." I looked at their blank expressions and realized they didn't understand English. So I thanked them in Russian, excused myself, and with barefooted dignity, I quietly walked over to the door and let myself out.

I strolled casually down the hall in my pretty pink cotton nightgown. (My mother believed in dressing in pretty things to sleep in, and I did too!) I entered my room and closed the door behind me. I still couldn't figure out how the hotel operator had repaired the phone in my room only to have my call come through in the room of another hotel guest. I decided not to ponder the possibility that the hotel mechanic hadn't fixed my phone but bugged it. It was, after all, a call to another country. I concluded that mix-ups were simply the Russian way, and I climbed into bed and fell asleep.

A few mornings later, on my way to breakfast, I walked across the cobblestones of Red Square and entered the National Hotel. I went directly up to the dining room, which was always crowded, but I found a small table and sat down. I began looking over the menu, which offered the usual breakfast fare, including something uniquely Russian that I enjoyed. It was prepared like a flat pancake, but while it lay flat, the chef would ply the pancake with a delicious jam and then sprinkle cooked chop meat on top. Carefully, the pancake with the jam and chopped meat was rolled up and placed as a long roll on your plate with scrambled eggs on the side. The Russians called this pancake dish a blinsky or blinski. I loved it and found it delicious.

Because I was a black girl in Moscow, Russians sitting nearby were surprised to see not only a foreigner, but also one of color, and they tended to stare. I was prepared for their stares, and as always, had brought a book with me to read. Once Russians latched onto someone they wanted to explore, they did so shamelessly and non-discretely.

You might look up and catch someone staring at you. That person never looked away, embarrassed, but simply continued to stare. I was used to this behavior.

When the waiter showed up, I placed my order, took out my book, and began to read. I knew the staring would go on for about ten minutes or so. I had developed a way of sensing when Russians had finally lost interest in me or had turned away to stare at something or someone else. But this morning, I became aware of another pair of eyes—not just curiously staring eyes, but eyes that actually bore into me! I ignored that person, deciding he was simply being rude.

I was determined to concentrate on my book, but when my breakfast arrived, I put the book down. With my peripheral vision, I saw the man who had been rudely staring stand and slip on his jacket. Curiosity prompted me to look at him as he passed my table to exit the dining room. In a matter of seconds and with his long stride, he was quickly at the exit doors, but I could see his face—and when I did, I was stunned! It was the stranger from the bus!

He was dressed differently—more casual, no big black coat this time. But it was our stranger!

Shocked, I wondered why he was still in Moscow. Hadn't he said we wouldn't be seeing him again, that he was leaving for the Republic of Georgia? And then I wondered why he sat staring at me instead of coming over to speak to me. My plan had been to ask him for that letter to his mother if I ever saw him again.

But my hopes of ever having that opportunity were lost again. The stranger had left the dining room after staring at me for ten long minutes, but he had passed by without even a glance in my direction. The hotel was huge. I couldn't run into the hall, not knowing which direction he'd gone. It took me a minute, but I collected myself and got over the surprise of seeing him again. Fewer than ten minutes later, Jason entered the dining room, and when he spotted me, he rushed over to my table.

Before he could say a word, I excitedly told him I had seen the stranger.

He laughed, telling me that only minutes ago, he too had met the Stranger in the hotel lobby. "The first thing he asked me to do was to apologize to you," Jason said.

"Really? Why?" I thought I knew why but waited for Jason to tell me.

"For not coming over to your table to speak to you," Jason said.

"I thought that was odd behavior, too," I confessed to Jason. "So, why didn't he?"

"He said he wasn't able to."

"Really, why not? I didn't see anyone trying to stop him."

Jason lowered his voice. "He told me he was being watched!"

"Being watched?" I too lowered my voice. "Who would be watching him—and why?" I wondered who would watch a man who had given up his country, family, and everything to become a citizen of the Soviet Union! Hadn't he already proven his loyalty by defecting? Was his loyalty to his new country still on trial after thirteen years?

"He didn't or couldn't say who was watching him," I heard Jason say. "But he said he was leaving for the Republic of Georgia in a few hours, and then he rushed out the door."

Now, let's fast forward ten years. I was no longer in the Soviet Union when I met an English couple in Connecticut who was visiting the States. Over lunch, I mentioned meeting this stranger on a bus in Moscow. I told them how the stranger had related how he had defected and how his dying mother pleaded with him to return home, but the stranger had been denied that trip. I told this English couple how the stranger handed me an envelope as we rode together on the bus—a letter he said he had written to his mother. But I also explained how just before getting off the bus, I instinctively handed the letter back to him. He had once explained that he felt previous letters had been intercepted.

Perhaps he was hoping I'd personally mail his letter once I was on American soil. But I had given it back. Now his dying mother would never know why her son had not returned home.

"You're very lucky you returned his letter," the Englishman said soberly.

"Really? But why? What about his dying mother?"

"Yes, the story about his mother, if true, is sad indeed," the Englishman said. "But only if this man was indeed an American who defected to Russian as he had described." I sensed this Englishman was going to poke holes in my long held theories. "But just suppose this stranger was really a Russian trained to look, act, and speak like an American?. Suppose, the letter was not a letter to dear Mom but a letter that contained government information about Russia. You did say that when he handed it to you, it was sealed."

I listened to this new point of view. It had never occurred to me the stranger might have been a fake. The impulsive, wayward son and his terminally ill mother were both very real to me. But I also knew being caught with a letter that contained government information was a serious matter. "So you think my concern was for a woman who never existed?" I inquired of my "Perhaps. But your humanitarian concern was commendable although perhaps misguided." He tried to soften those words. "Unfortunately, Russia is a country where things are not always what they seem. This dying woman, his mother, may have existed only in the mind of the stranger—an intriguing story perhaps only meant to ensnare the listener. So, sorry, my dear."

"I'm grateful for your perspective," I said, giving his words serious thought. "I guess it's time I let the stranger and his story go." They all agreed. "I thought in returning the letter, I had somehow let a dying woman down, but now I'm glad I returned his letter to him before I stepped off the bus." I sighed a heavy sigh. "I realize my good deed, as innocent as it was intended to be, could have seriously eroded my future."

Was the story the Stranger relayed fact or fiction? I'll never know. But I have learned that wearing your heart on your sleeve in a country like Russia can prove to be a hazard to your health!

CHAPTER 11

Take the A Train

During the day, if you strolled down Moscow's busy streets, you could hear Russian music played from a variety of shops. One such Russian tune was heard everywhere you went in Moscow, and it was loved by all.

American composers wrote compositions in tribute to cities like Chicago, New York, or San Francisco, and so it was true of two Russian composers Vasily Soljev-Sedoy and Michael Matusovsky, one of whom was born in the city of Leningrad. The two decided to name their composition "Leningrad Nights."

But the title of "Leningrad Nights" didn't stick, so another title, "Moscow Suburban Nights," was thought catchy. But then "Midnight in Moscow" was felt a better choice until someone suggested "Moscow Nights," which stuck! "Moscow Nights" even became a hit song in China! It has been translated into many languages. But the version recorded by the caressing voice of Vladimir Troshin sold millions, and the rest is history.

It seemed no one could get enough of "Moscow Nights." It could be heard as instrumental or vocal, and both versions have a beautiful, lilting, wistful quality heightened by the infusion of haunting mandolins. Even today, I can sing its lovely refrain.

But without a doubt, Russians had a great fondness for American music, especially jazz. There must have been many a jazz spot in Moscow, but one such hangout for both Russians and foreign visitors was an eclectic jazz spot called the Praga.

The Praga had the feel and ambiance of a nightclub in Harlem, New York because it was hot, steamy, and exciting. Every time I went to the Praga, it was always crowded with a happy crowd speaking many languages. The music was always live, the drinks nonstop, and the food hot and delectable.

People were friendly, and you actually heard laughter, something seldom heard on Moscow streets. Russians on the streets of Moscow wanted to be anonymous and not draw attention to themselves. Big Brother in the guise of the KGB or the Secret Police seemed to lurk around every corner. But at the Praga, Russians let their hair down and gathered to meet, greet, and enjoy themselves.

One night, as I entered The Praga with the lovely "Moscow Nights" still ringing in my ears, I made my way over to the table, where a few friends were waiting. The trio was dishing out some great Russian tune when the pianist suddenly began playing the first few cords of an American jazz classic, Duke Ellington's "Take the A Train!"

Because I heard only Russian music all day, this American tune seemed oddly out of place. Startled to hear an American tune in the midst of a Russian crowd, I immediately turned toward the trio. As I did so, I looked across the room and into the eyes of the handsome Russian pianist who with an impish grin sat looking directly at me! He was a young guy with dark hair that was slicked back in the style of the late 1940s. He was perhaps in his early or late thirties, and he wore a black suit and white shirt and tie. It was apparent as he stared at me that he was getting a kick out of musically catching me off guard by inserting the Duke's classic in the middle of a Russian number.

For a second or so, I stood there, wondering if he had intentionally played "Take the A Train" as a kind of greeting to me. But as I noted the grin on his face, I knew without a doubt that he had found a way to greet me across that crowded floor.

He was very clever, and from that night on, whenever I entered the Praga, the pianist would find a way of inserting a brief Ellington cord. I would turn to him and smile, wave, and blow him a kiss! Then together, across the expanse of that restaurant floor, we shared a private smile at our tuneful way of communicating.

But my ear was forced to adjust to hearing "Take the A Train" in the midst of a club filled with Russian jazz. Perhaps it was the difference in the instruments used, the cadence, or the beat that my American ear had to adjust to.

But on that night, as on other nights, I stood in that happy, chatty, crowded place and I looked over at the pianist smiling at me across the restaurant floor. The waiters dashed to and fro, serving drinks of muted hues on shiny silver trays while steaming platters of hot foods left trails of culinary fragrances. There was, if only for a moment, just the two of us—me and that Russian piano player. His hands were never at rest, constantly pounding out great music as we stole a smile and a brief wave in greeting to each other.

I regret that I never met him or never heard his voice, nor he mine. On one of those nights, I should have made my way through that milling crowd and approached him and shook those marvelous hands. I mistakenly thought there would be time to do that later. But for a brief moment in time, the Duke's music had united us.

I can still see him sitting at his piano, a slim, handsome man dressed neatly in his black suit, white shirt, and tie, filling the night with his glorious sound while uniquely slipping in a few bars of "Take the A Train" in greeting to a black girl in Moscow.

CHAPTER 12

The Woman Who Persisted

We Americans had been in Moscow three weeks when we had a desire for a taste of Chinese food. We were told The Peking Restaurant in Moscow was a good bet. We took a taxi, and as we entered the restaurant, we were greeted by bright lights, bright orange dragons, and Chinese snakes painted in brilliant red, yellow, green, and black colors. Overhead were at least twenty floating Chinese lanterns. The restaurant was lit like a Christmas tree. The music was loud, and the lights seemed too bright, but the Peking Restaurant was crowded.

A hostess led us to a large table and handed each of us menus. To our dismay, there were no pictures of food selections. Plus, the menu was written in two languages—Chinese and Russian—with no English for the English visitor. We were in a fix as to what to order. We considered asking the waitress for her recommendations, but she spoke only Chinese and Russian. She was very busy and had little time for taking us through the menu. When she came back to take our orders, we decided because the place was so crowded and people obviously enjoyed the food, everything on the menu had to be good. We randomly selected our dinner by ordering by the numbers. With the ordering done, we sat back, looked around the place, and took in the crowd.

Dancing was a favorite pastime in Moscow. If there was a spacious floor and music, Russians didn't waste an opportunity to dance. I was at first surprised to see two men, usually big muscular guys, dancing smoothly together. Homosexuals were rarely if ever seen in Moscow. Although homosexuality existed in Russia, those of that persuasion kept a low profile. But men dancing together was explained to be an exercise of convenience that simply allowed heterosexual men to move around the dance floor and scan the crowd for women they might later want to ask to dance. Two men would dance together because why waste good music standing on the sidelines when you could be on the dance floor with somebody, even another guy?

Two men dancing together paid little attention to each other. While they danced, one guy would look in one direction, and his dancing partner would look in the opposite direction, each scanning the crowd for a woman of his choice. Two guys with their hands held high and bodies never touching expertly moved around the floor. Finally, as the music ended, one or both guys might have singled out a woman he'd like to ask to dance. Dancing with another guy was considered a dance of convenience.

A young blond woman came over to me after I had placed my order with the waitress. The blond was attractive and slender, at least my height. She was wearing light gray slacks and a matching gray short-sleeved blouse. She spoke to me in Russian. Because I was in Moscow as a model, I had become accustomed to being approached by Russians who would compliment me. I was also often stopped in Sokolniki Park and asked for my autograph; it was also very nice. Assuming this blond woman had said something complementary to me, I thanked her, and she turned and walked away.

Of all the restaurants I'd been to in Moscow, I liked this restaurant the least. The lighting was too harsh, the music too loud, and the decor too gaudy; the verdict about the food was yet to be determined. We Americans tried to talk above the blaring music, and as we did so, I saw the same blond woman coming toward me again. She looked me in the eye, smiled at me politely, and spoke to me again. "Thank you," I said in Russian, and she turned and walked away.

The food finally arrived. We had each ordered a different dish. My plate was large and filled with a gray liquid with some seaweed-looking plant floating in that watery, gray paste. This wasn't American Chinese food. I laughed to myself. That's what I think we wanted—American

Chinese food. This food might have been too authentic. But we knew we would get no American Chinese-style food at this Peking restaurant.

The blond woman came over again. I was puzzled by her repeated trips to speak to me and repeating the same words each time. I had already thanked her, but here she was again, standing in front of me, saying what I think she had said before. Again, I smiled and politely thanked her. But this time, she refused to leave. I looked at her, and now I was really concerned because this woman just wouldn't go away.

Someone at my table asked, "You know what she's asking you?"

"No, I guess not," I replied, perplexed.

"She's asking you for a dance."

"You're kidding!" I said.

I'd noticed men as they danced together, but I had not paid any attention to women dancing together. Finally understanding and admiring her persistence, I stood and indicated I would follow her. Once we were on the dance floor, she took the lead and made me appear to be a better dancer than I really was. As we circled the dance floor, I was glad she had been persistent because of all this restaurant lacked, dancing with her somehow made the evening worthwhile!

CHAPTER 13

The Man Upstairs

The last fashion show of the day would end at about 7:00 p.m., which was a perfect time to decide where to have dinner. But as would often be the case, we would leave our trailer dressing room and find ourselves face-to-face with Russians waiting to talk. It was always exciting to meet Russians who wanted to get to know us. They sometimes just wanted to thank us for being in Moscow and being in the show.

On this particular night in early August, three Russian brothers were waiting as we models emerged from our trailer. They told us their ages; the eldest was nineteen, his brother was seventeen, and the youngest boy was almost sixteen. They were good-looking boys and nicely and casually dressed. The older two spoke English well enough to be understood by us. They each spoke some English, with the youngest brother speaking English sparingly; he was not yet as proficient as his brothers.

They explained that they lived in Moscow in an apartment they shared with their parents who were away at a Communist weekend retreat. They were hoping a few of us would consider having dinner with them at their apartment to have an open discussion about politics. The dinner only needed reheating because it was already prepared.

Up to that point, I had yet to see the inside of a Russian apartment. Of course, with neighbors who spied on each other, Russians entertaining foreigners was rare. But these three brothers seemed unconcerned, and I felt this to be a golden opportunity to satisfy my curiosity about what the inside of a Russian apartment looked like. Their apartment was in a high-rise building in Moscow. Inviting Americans as guests seemed a rebellious act when their parents were active Communist Party members. But for them, it was perhaps also an experiment in whether we might be able to share a meal, enjoy conversation, and possibly explore common ground. Six models from the show, including myself, accepted their invitation.

Outside of Sokolniki Park, we hailed a taxi, and the brothers gave our taxi driver their address while they took a second cab. Less than ten minutes later, we were in front of their apartment building. Quietly, we took the elevator to the eighth floor. The eldest brother opened the door, and we all filed in. It was a small two-bedroom apartment. With the elevator, the upkeep of the building, and modern kitchen appliances, it was clearly a luxury apartment. I think we Americans were all struck by the obvious plushness of the furnishings. There were two stuffed floral arm chairs, flowered throws on the plush sofa, and patterned drapes on the windows. On the floors were scattered floral fringed rugs—some oval and others round. Pictures hung on white painted walls depicting country scenes, but on an end table were family pictures of the boys when they were young with smiling parents and an older couple we were told were their grandparents.

My overall impression of the apartment was that it was pastel, featuring flowers of soft pinks, pale yellows, delicate greens, and sky blues. With four men in the family, a father and three sons, it seemed the decor was decidedly feminine, and the one woman among them had the last word on decorating their home.

With three strapping sons, we wondered how they all fit into such small rooms, but evidently they all did. Apparently, although small, this was the kind of apartment awarded to faithful members of the Communist Party.

Their living and dining room also had a long rectangular table covered in a floral table cloth and plastic placemats, but the table caused the room to appear cramped. The table served the family of five well because it was where they shared meals together. Perhaps the other reason such a large conference-like table was needed was for meetings with party members.

We sat at their table, and the brothers placed a variety of fruits, meats, breads, and vegetables for us to dine on. I noticed that even while dining in restaurants, vegetables were not fully grown, or at least they had not grown to the size of those we were accustomed to in the United States. Perhaps this was because of different agricultural methods used in farming. The Soviet Union was an industrial nation, and although farming was needed to provide food for the populace, some agricultural methods used in other counties were not practiced in Russia.

A small roasted chicken on a platter was placed before us. They were generous in what they offered us. This was no reflection on them as hosts, but I think our group ate sparingly because their offerings looked so meager in size.

It also became apparent that the brothers had been raised to think Russia was superior to other nations. "No one country—including America—could win an arms race against Russia."

"What makes you so sure?" we asked.

"Because Russia fully concentrates on producing weapons. You Americans think about luxury cars or fashions, silly stuff like that."

"Where do you get your information?" we asked, and there was a moment of silence. "Russian news?" we asked again. "Why do you think so many Russians listen to Radio Free Europe? You can't even trust your news media to report the news accurately. How can you seriously discuss any current events if you're only fed what your government wants you to believe?"

That was a hard blow, but they took it well—almost. "We trust our Russian news media," one brother said, crestfallen. You could tell they really didn't.

We continued our attack. "You're not allowed to travel outside of Russia. What is your government afraid you'll see?"

The brothers were stumped again. They could see no reason for their inability to travel outside of Russia. And as though to make up for that infraction, one brother stated proudly "Our government gives all its people paid annual vacations."

"Yes," we said, "but not outside of Russia!"

There was silence from the brothers. "Russia is beautiful," one brother proclaimed.

"We enjoy our vacations along the Black Sea," another brother acknowledged.

"But you're right; we still would like to visit other countries!" the eldest brother lamented.

"We would never defect," one brother stated with surety. The other two did not back him up. "What greater country is there than Russia?" the second eldest brother asked, giving his older brother a cross look.

I felt his question indicated a sense of false bravado because they knew from cradle to grave that Russians were to remain in Russia. "How can you speak about what you don't know?" we asked. Again, there was silence. I waited for the subject of race relations to begin, but the Russian brothers seemed to have no interest in that topic.

Finally, we took a break. I wanted some fresh air, so I stepped through a door that led to their balcony, which was large enough for two chairs. I sat and breathed deeply of the night air. I felt the pleasant evening breeze and looked up at the vast dark blue sky overhead. Eventually, the youngest of the brothers came out and joined me. We were sitting in silence for a few minutes when I jokingly said, "You know, the skies over New York City have the same stars overhead as does Moscow."

He was quiet for a minute, perhaps processing what I'd said. Eventually, he laughed, but then he turned serious. "Do you believe in the man upstairs?" he inquired.

"Who?" I asked, not sure I understood his question or whom he was referring to.

"You know," he insisted while pointing to the sky, "the man upstairs!"

"Oh." I understood. "You mean God, right? That man upstairs?" I was surprised he was familiar of the term.

"Yes, yes!" the young teen said as he impatiently nodded his head. It seemed he wanted to avoid saying the word God, so he asked me again with greater urgency, "Do you believe in the man upstairs?" He wanted no discussion, only my answer.

"Yes," I said as I looked at him. "I believe in God; do you?"

"No!" he shouted vehemently as he nearly spat out the word.

"What do you believe in?" I asked, wondering what a sixteen-year-old Russian teen believed.

"I believe in people," he said decisively. Then without saying another word, he left and joined the others inside.

I remained sitting on the balcony, basking in the quiet left behind by this intense Russian boy. I wondered if his faith in people would serve him well.

Finally, I rejoined the others, as it was getting late. Minutes later, we were saying good night, shaking hands, and being thanked for coming. We thanked them for being so gracious, and we left.

I wondered if Russia would one day be too big for these brothers or too small. Khrushchev came from a long line of dictators who were anti-religion. Karl Marx called religion the "opiate of the people," and his assessment continued with Joseph Stalin.

During that time, Premiere Khrushchev conducted anti-religious campaigns throughout his country. The topic of religion was intolerable to Khrushchev, and he constantly searched for ways to prove there was no God. A few years later, he would latch on to an addition to his anti-religious rhetoric. Cosmonaut Yuri Gagarin, the celebrated first man in space, went into orbit, and upon Gagarin's return, Premiere Khrushchev asked him if he'd seen God while he was in space.

It is claimed the cosmonaut told Khrushchev, "I did not see God while I was in space." But records dispute whether Gagarin ever spoke those words to Khrushchev. As a matter of fact, it was known that Gagarin arranged to have his daughters baptized before he boarded his spaceship.

Bill Davis, a handsome and strapping Africa American who spoke eight languages fluently and a longtime United States government employee stationed in Russia, invited me and models Norma Jean Johnson and Gil Noble to attend Sunday morning services at a two hundred-year-old church called the Central Baptist Church in Moscow. This church was the only functioning Baptist church in the state.

It was a small church nestled between larger structures on an austere street in Moscow not far from Red Square. Knowing Russia's stance on religion made me want to attend this church just to stand among its faithful. How the Central Baptist Church of Moscow remained actively functioning through a turbulent two hundred-year history is truly a mystery of faith.

Joseph Stalin had a five-year plan (1932–1937) to rid Russia of all religious expression, but the church survived. It was declared that the concept of God would disappear if more churches were closed and more priests and pastors were persecuted, but the church survived. Propaganda mills churned out stories that Baptists in Russia were really American spies who ate children; these stories appealed to non-believers, but the church survived. The Soviets forced people to work on Sundays so they would be unable to attend church, but the church survived.

Those who dared attend Christmas and Easter services invited a prison sentence, but some defied the government, and the church survived. The twenty-fifth and twenty-sixth of December were proclaimed days of industrialization on which the whole country would celebrate by working. And those who did not go to work but attended church instead were arrested for truancy. But through all of that, the church survived.

Those in this congregation were devoted to their religious ideals— look what they had endured! Even children were used in this anti-religion campaign; their assignment was to go home and convert family members to atheism. If a child returned to school with names of those who had not converted, those family members were arrested. Members of the Central Baptist Church in Moscow, where the constant threat was imprisonment, needed strong, unwavering faith.

We arrived in time for the 11:00 a.m. service, and the church was already packed. The fact that the church was crowded should have come as no surprise because large numbers of churches had been closed down due to Khrushchev's anti-religious campaigns. Russia's faithful, on a quest to find a place to worship, crowded into Central Baptist Church.

The number of attendees reminded me of church attendance during the Easter or Christmas holidays in the States. Americans who had not attended church all year attended in record numbers on those two important religious holidays. But this Sunday in Russia was no holiday. Soviet citizens attended church in record numbers every Sunday because the spiritual need to attend was there.

The church was crowded with the elderly and the very young. They invited us in, and although every seat was filled, those attending offered their seats to us. Hymns were sung, prayers were read, and the minister gave a sermon that fed the spiritual and emotional needs of the congregation.

Unfortunately, the campaign against religion would continue. If you were in your twenties or thirties, you could be arrested because you attended church. So on this Sunday morning, as I looked around, I saw men and women who had managed to bring a child or two with them. Grandparents found a way to expose their grandchildren to a tiny measure of religion for a few hours each week. By doing so, they hoped to keep religious practices alive and pass the religious torch. Despite religious persecution, religious communities in Russia not only exist, but also thrive.

Every two weeks, we models were given two days off. On one excursion, my colleagues and I took a train from Moscow and visited the town of

Zagorst, now known as Sergeyev Posad, which was founded in 1345. It is the spiritual center of Russian Orthodox Christianity. The trip was about forty-five miles from Moscow.

We walked around Zagorsk, admiring the beautiful Holy Trinity Lavra Monastery, the exterior of which is painted a gleaming white. If you cast your eyes upward, you see the onion-shaped, gold-painted domes that are peacock blue with golden stars. It was strange to see an entire town devoted to religion when a few miles away, in Moscow, the practice of religion was nearly completely forbidden.

As tourists, we tried taking pictures of the beaded priests in their long black robes and black fitted caps, but they shyly scurried away while putting their hands up to protect their faces from being photographed.

Beautiful St. Basil's was built on Moscow's Red Square sometime between 1555 and 1561. Napoleon Bonaparte was said to have been so infatuated with St. Basil's that he wanted to transport the entire building back to France. Luckily for Moscow, he was unable to find a way to move this unique structure from where it stood. For some reason, Napoleon wanted to burn the church down, but fortunately he was unsuccessful, mainly because of a heavy rainfall that doused the flames. St. Basil's history is fascinating and varied, but religion was not meant to reside within its walls. In 1923, St. Basil's was forced to open as a museum and stands as such today.

CHAPTER 14

All Black People Can Dance?

Ernst and Hans, both from Finland, were in Russia to cover the American National Exhibition in Moscow for Paris Match magazine. Hans was tall, Ernst was short, and both were friendly and humorous. After watching them take pictures and write their articles about the fashion show, they asked if I would dine with them at the Baku. The Baku was a large Georgian restaurant in Moscow. It had a reputation as a restaurant with an excellent cuisine and a friendly environment.

I returned to my hotel to dress for our dinner date. I selected a conservative summer suit made of raw silk with a light black and white glen plaid pattern. The jacket was waist-length and boxy with three-quarter-length sleeves and a casual buttonless front. The skirt was knee-length and straight with a little split at the hem in the back. Under the jacket, I wore a soft knit, sleeveless white blouse. My shoes were black patent leather slingbacks with pencil-thin, three-inch heels. I carried my favorite little black purse.

At the appointed time, Hans and Ernst called my room to tell me they were in the hotel lobby. I joined them, and we immediately climbed into one of the taxis that was parked outside the Leningradskya and headed to the Baku.

The restaurant's front doors were elegant, and both men held the doors open for me. We entered and faced a large dining room with highly polished hardwood floors. There were more than sixty round dinner tables covered with crisp white cotton tablecloths on which were napkins and utensils in preparation for the evening crowd. We were early, so the room was empty, but as we walked through, I noticed that there was an elevated bandstand and a large area of the floor reserved for dancing.

Hans, Ernst, and I wanted to dine in the smaller, more cozy and private back room. As we entered, we felt the warmth and intimacy of this dining room because of its dark-paneled wood grain walls, elegant brocade drapes, and a large dimly lit crystal chandelier.

A waiter escorted us to a table ample in size for the three of us. Other diners sat nearby, already enjoying their meals. We were given menus from which we placed our orders.

While waiting, we chatted; the three of us always seemed to have much to talk about. We joked, which Hans was very good at. The waiter placed the plates of food on our table. Everything looked delicious, and he quietly walked away. Only seconds later, he returned, proudly displaying a bottle of wine that he explained was a gift from a nearby table. We looked over at the table where four Georgian men sat with their wine glasses raised in greeting. Hastily, the waiter filled our glasses, and then we too raised our glasses, thanking the men for their excellent gift.

To our surprise, a little while later, one of the men spoke openly about former Russian ruler Joseph Stalin. Stalin, who was also a Georgian, was declared by this man to be a disgrace to the Georgian people. Those sitting at his table agreed with this assessment of Stalin, a man hated but also loved by many.

Hans, Ernst, and I listened but knew better than to lend a voice to their discussion. Stalin, who appeared the picture of health, surprised his nation when he died suddenly at the age of seventy-three. His body lay in a mausoleum outside of Red Square. Every day for the previous six years, lines of Russians patiently waited to view the body of their former leader. Feelings about Stalin ran deep and were complex.

Daily, Russians lined up to view Stalin's body, and it seems many did so out of a genuine love for their deceased leader. But it was widely known that many stood in line because it was politically correct to be seen at Stalin's mausoleum. Millions breathed a sigh of relief when Stalin died, because with his death, his reign of terror ended. Yet despite the knowledge that Stalin had killed millions, many Russians cried bitterly that they were now leaderless and had lost a beloved father.

The band in the outer dining room of the Baku began to play. Ernst, Hans, and I left our table and walked over to the doorway, where we stood listening. The room that was empty when we first arrived was now completely filled with sophisticated diners. After a few minutes, the bandleader brought the music to a halt, flipped through some sheets of music, and turned and pointed a finger in our direction. "Was he pointing at us?" I asked of Ernst and Hans. "What could he want?"

"I think he wants you," they whispered.

Shocked, I asked, "Why me?"

"You might have to go over and ask," was their reply.

"Really?" I asked, mystified. I inhaled deeply as I contemplated the long walk to the bandstand.

Stepping slowly and carefully on the polished floors, I made my way to the bandstand. As I walked, I was conscious of the *click-clack* noise made by my high-heeled shoes against the wooden floor. All chatter ceased as I made my way toward the band leader. I knew in a city where people of color were rarely seen, this audience was open and honest in its curiosity. The women, I thought, had to be admiring my outfit and my shoes, amazed at how strong my pencil-thin heels had to be to support my weight without snapping in half.

I finally reached the bandstand, and from his lofty position, the bandleader looked down at me. I noticed he neglected to greet me, but instead he said, "You dance!"

For a second, I simply stared at him. I wondered if he had heard the old but untrue adage that all black people had a natural ability to dance. "Dance?" I asked out loud. If I wasn't so surprised by his command, I might have laughed. I was truly no dancer. My second-grade teacher would tell you I had two left feet, and through the years, that had not changed. But I was also wearing a two-piece suit with a straight skirt that was totally inappropriate for dancing. I knew Ginger Rogers would never dance in a suit! Wasn't the band leader aware of those movies with Fred Astaire and Ginger Rogers? Hadn't he noticed that Ginger always wore long dresses with full skirts?

"We play 'Rock Around the Clock'; you dance!" He spoke with all the charm of a drill sergeant giving his troops an order. He turned away, not giving me a chance to reply. I knew he cared not what I thought because instead, he gave his full attention to the band, and with a backward glance at me, he commanded again, "Dance!"

I stood there with my back to the diners. Should I turn and walk away, into the safety of the smaller dining room? Or should I show him that I am an American who was not afraid of a flimsy challenge like dancing solo for the first time in my life unrehearsed and in front of a live audience? I looked up again at his back and thought, *Why not?* From this trip, I stored up memories that would last me a lifetime, and this night would be one of those unforgettable memories!

My one advantage was that I was at least familiar with "Rock Around the Clock." The piece had been a hit by Bill Haley and the Comets years earlier. To my mind, it was definitely not a piece for a solo dance debut, but as they say, you take what you get!

Having made up my mind, I turned and faced the diners as the band played a rendition of "Rock Around the Clock" that was as fast as a runaway train. I began to move lightly across the dance floor. I had the floor all to myself; it was huge, and I wished I knew some fancy footwork. But I knew how to dip, bend, and lift my arms up in time with the music. Luckily for me, I couldn't see the faces of my audience as they sat silently watching me in the darkened room.

I could feel the freedom of that spacious dance floor as I raised my arms and made careful but hopefully graceful turns, mindful of the slippery floor. Oh, to have worn comfortable slippers instead of dress shoes with three-inch heels. But who knew this night would call for an unplanned dance recital?

I danced on, inventing steps in keeping with the restriction of my corporate-style suit. I turned this way and that, moving my arms, crossing my feet, and spinning around carefully. The band played on, and I danced for more than fifteen minutes, inventing and reinventing steps, bending, turning, always mindful of the limitations of my outfit, my heels, the floors, and my lack of dancing expertise. Was the silent crowd amazed, entertained, enthralled, or bewildered?

Tonight would prove again that dancing was not in my DNA. If this band leader ever approached another person of color to dance for him again, I hope he would check his or her credentials first! Whoever spread that rumor that all black people could dance should first see me!

But exactly like Ginger Rogers being joined by Fred Astaire, I was joined by a tall, slender Russian gentleman in a conservative light gray suit.

He elegantly placed one arm around my waist while taking my right hand into his. He then skillfully guided me back toward the band stand. In a few easy steps, we were staring up at the bandleader, who finally brought the music to an ear-splitting halt.

My dashing Russian hero handed the bandleader one hundred rubles (about ten dollars), a tip the bandleader seemed grateful to receive. My Russian gentleman friend turned to me and bowed, then to the audience, where we bowed together, and the diners broke into applause. Then this elegant fellow glided me over to where Ernst and Hans stood waiting. Once he delivered me, he graciously wished all of us a good night in Russian, and like the hero in Hollywood films, he smartly strode away!

Ernst, Hans, and I returned to our table, where I received congratulations on, if nothing more, my endurance and determination to stay the course. Now I was being toasted by those in the dining room. As I raised my glass high, I smiled, thinking, *Who would have thought it? Most especially not my second-grade teacher, would not have believed that her worst seven-year-old dance student had thrilled—well that may be taking it too far, perhaps I should say I entertained—a huge audience years later in a night club in Moscow!*

CHAPTER 15

Lost in St. Petersburg

I had a few days off from performing in the fashion show. On a sunny day, four models and I took a train to St. Petersburg. We wanted to visit this thriving city and the Peterhauf, or House of Peter. We arrived in St. Petersburg. Somehow we ended up at the wrong hotel—but how beautiful it was!

While the group was at the front desk, hoping to get information on how to get to our rightful hotel where we had reservations, all the luggage was on the floor in front of the desk, including my weekender bag that contained my money and passport. But I was mesmerized by the gleaming chandeliers, intricate patterns on the carpets, and hand-painted wallpaper. I wandered off into a large parlor room that seemed to go back to a faraway time in Russian history. When I emerged from the parlor room, to my horror my entire group was gone, as well as all the luggage!

"Where did they go? I asked.

"They took the bus," the Russian lady said.

"Which bus?"

"The bus to the Astor Hotel."

"Where can I get that bus?"

"It stops right outside in front of this hotel."

"Thank you." I walked away, but then I realized I had no money or passport—and Russia is the last place you want to be without identification! How could I take the bus? I didn't have my fare, which was one little kopec! (A kopec was a small, round, copper-looking coin with less value than an American penny.)

Desperate, I looked around and saw an elderly white lady walking in my direction. I had heard her speak, so I knew she was American. I approached her, and although embarrassed, I had to ask her if she had any coins to spare. "Excuse me," I said. "My friends have gone off to the Astor hotel, and they took my bag that contained my wallet. I need one kopec to take the bus to catch up to them."

"My dear," she said, "I am visiting from Michigan, but I am leaving Russia tonight."

"You're leaving tonight?" I was going to ask if she had enjoyed her stay, but before I could, she extended her hand. "I don't need so many coins to take home with me," she said. "Here, take what you want."

Grateful to her, I took two kopecs. "Thank you," I said.

"My dear, find your friends. But be very careful."

"Thank you so much." She had advised me to be careful. Without any identification in a country like Russia, I felt an individual who was also all alone could disappear without a trace. Heck, even with an ID, I had that same sinking feeling; you could no longer exist. "Have a safe trip home!" I shouted to the American as I rushed out, hoping to catch the next bus to the Astor Hotel.

Outside, the bus I needed was standing there with its doors open, so I simply stepped on board. The bus was crowded, but I was happy to stand near the front door. As the bus moved through the streets of St. Petersburg, I looked out the window and saw four people rushing down the crowded Russian street! "Let me off!" I shouted to the driver. The bus stopped and opened its doors, and I stepped off!

"Jackie!" they all shouted when they saw me. I fell into their arms, and we all hugged.

"We didn't realize you weren't with us until we got to the Astor. Were you afraid?" Dorothy, one of the models, asked.

"Me?" I asked. "No! When you're from Brooklyn, getting lost in Russia is a piece of cake!" We all laughed, but I confess that finding myself in a strange city in Russia, not knowing the language and with no money to get back to where I started from or passport to prove my identity was not a comfortable situation to find myself in!

CHAPTER 16

A Jamaican in Moscow

It was an early August afternoon when I met a gentleman from Jamaica, West Indies. He stood alone just outside our trailer. He was small in stature and neatly dressed in a suit that was nicely tailored to fit his slender frame. I guessed he was in his early fifties. "Hi," I said immediately. I smiled, sensing for some reason that I should let him approach me first.

"Hello," he said. He seemed somehow cautious, as though if I had rebuffed him, he would have turned and walked away.

"Did you see the show?" I asked, standing at a distance, letting him warm up to me.

"Yes, I saw it, and enjoyed it very much!" he replied shyly. As I looked at him, something about him belied the fact that there was a toughness about him.

"Good," I said. "And your name?"

"Oh, I'm sorry," he said, slightly embarrassed. "My name is Bob, short for Robert—Robert Robinson." I gave him a look, wondering what his story might be. How had he ended up in the Soviet Union?

"Hi, Bob." I extended my hand to shake his. "My next show is not for another couple hours. Care to take a walk around the park?" I asked, somehow feeling he would be open to the idea.

"Yes," he said, and he walked beside me.

"So, are you on vacation in Moscow?" I asked him, and finally he laughed!

"Vacation, did you say? Oh, no! I've lived in Moscow for twenty-seven years, and believe me, it has seldom felt like a vacation."

I stopped short, and I looked at him. "Did you say twenty-seven years?"

"Twenty-seven years." His response was somber.

I had heard him right. Naturally, questions were spinning around in my brain. I saw an empty bench and headed toward it. I sat, and Bob did too. "Can I ask you to tell me a little about yourself?" I asked Bob.

"I was born in Jamaica, West Indies." Bob told me.

"Wow! Jamaica—you're a long way from home! How did that happen?" I couldn't believe how bold I was. I almost felt that if I didn't learn about him today, he might disappear.

Bob began slowly speaking. "When I was a young man, I wanted to study engineering, so I found a University in Cuba and earned my engineering degree. With my degree in hand, I set my sights on Detroit, Michigan, where I wanted to work for Ford Motor Company." Bob spoke easily, and I found his voice easy on the ear. "I wasted no time making plans to get to Detroit!"

"Well, why not?" I said. "You had your credentials in hand; nothing could stop you now!"

"My mother, bless her—we left Jamaica, packed up everything we owned, and traveled to Michigan. When we got there, the weather was cold, so different from my beloved Jamaica." He smiled, remembering. "My brother was already living in a small apartment in Detroit, so my mother and I moved in with him. I immediately went to Ford and applied for a job as an engineer. They promptly turned me down."

"But why?" I asked. I wanted to believe his degree should have opened doors for him, not close them.

"It was explained to me," Bob continued, "that because Ford had never hired a black engineer before, they could not hire me," he explained casually.

"Come on, they had to start with someone—why not you?"

"You would think so. My mother and I discussed the options. We had come so far. There was no turning back, and I needed a job! The only job available for me as a black man at Ford was that of a maintenance worker—and I swallowed my pride and took it!"

I knew I saw a toughness in him. "But your degree was in engineering!" Like he needed to be reminded. "What an insult!"

"No, no insult. Now I was on the inside!" Bob replied jubilantly.

I looked at my new friend with admiration. "Many would have walked away—let their dream die."

"I took that job in maintenance, and every day, I reported to work with a positive attitude." Bob worked for only a few months when he began offering suggestions that eventually solved some engineering problem the crew might have been working on. After a while, the engineering crew began relying on Bob's input.

He always reported early, and one morning, he found the engineers were unable to go further on a project and wanted to hear Bob's opinion. After he added his suggestion to the mix, the project was on its way to a final solution. After a few more collaborations of this kind, Bob said, "I think you guys need to hire me as an engineer." There were no objections. He was now working as an engineer. He had been a maintenance worker a total of seven months!

"Wow, you did it! You must have felt pretty good about that!"

"That evening, when I told my mother and brother, there was joy in our house! They knew I had achieved my dream—really my mother's dream, too, because she had been with me every step of the way."

"You had a special relationship with your mom, didn't you?"

"She was a very special person, always positive and encouraging. Then in 1927, several Russians visited Ford Motor Company. They wanted Ford to assign engineers to teach Russians how to develop automobiles at their plant in Moscow. I and six white engineers were chosen. I loved the assignment! I now had the opportunity to do the work I loved and travel! While working in Moscow, I would receive an excellent salary. I was doing what I loved, and I knew I'd be home at the end of a year."

"That was so long ago," I said, "but you stayed in Russia for the job?"

He didn't answer. He rubbed his brow and then turned to me and said, "You've asked a very good question. No, I didn't stay because of the job."

"Then why? Why did you not return to Detroit where you had family, a mother and a brother waiting?"

"Believe me, I wanted to return home, but situations didn't allow it."

"Situations? What situations?"

"My contract with the plant was for two years. Now remember, I arrived in 1927. Two years later, it was 1929. We all know what happened in 1929—the stock market had crashed. I would never have believed it, but America was devastated. People who had once been successful were now jumping out of windows, standing on bread lines. Companies were folding. No one was working. My job at Ford was gone. If I left Russia to return to America, I would, as a black man, be the last hired—if I was even hired at all—and the first one fired. I had a mother to support. I needed a job."

"Oh, I remember reading about the Depression, the bread lines, the suicides," I said to Bob.

"Yes, and then my boss at the plant here in Moscow said I could keep my job if I wanted it."

"If you wanted it!" We both laughed.

"If I wanted it! I was so happy to have a job. I was a good worker; they still needed my know-how. I accepted, but I should have known there was a catch."

"What was the catch?" I asked.

"To keep my job, I had to give up my citizenship!" Bob looked at me.

"Give up your citizenship? Wow, a heavy price for a job. But it was either that or breadlines, I guess."

"I had known others in Russia who had given up their citizenship, but when they needed to leave, they were allowed to leave," Bob explained. "I thought I would leave Russia when things improved in America. But for me, it was different. I was never allowed to leave. I was a good worker, so they didn't want to let me go."

"Oh, man!"

"So I have been in the Soviet Union almost three decades with every door being closed in my face."

"But how could they?"

"Oh, they can, but I've never stopped trying. Naturally, I tried during my mother's illness, her eventual death, her burial—and I, her eldest son, was absent from it all. I'll never forgive this government for that." There was an edge of bitterness in his voice. "Even the excellent salary was greatly cut now that I am no longer an American citizen and now that the Russian government is footing the bill. I have been forced to get a second job to make ends meet."

"No kidding?"

"Kidding? I wish I was kidding. I was raised loving concerts, the opera, the ballet, and a second job allows me to enjoy my love of the arts. I am lucky, because since I am forced to be here, at least there is culture for me to enjoy!"

"Yes, lucky you, I guess. But still, the price for that seems high," I said.

Although he had had opportunities to marry, he said he never planned to marry a Russian woman. He knew of marriages between Russian men and women resulted in one spouse spying on the other, supplying the KGB with information about his or her mate. Bob felt, had he married and been blessed with children, that children would forever bind him to Russia. He also knew if he had an opportunity to leave Russia, he could never leave his children behind.

"Bob, your life has been fascinating. Can we talk again tomorrow? The second fashion show will be stating soon." I stood, and Bob did too.

"I'll walk you back," he said, and we started moving toward the trailer that I would enter to begin preparation for the next show. "Thank you for listening. I can't trust too many people," Bob said.

"I can certainly understand why!" I said. There were too many garden-variety spies in Moscow willing to sell someone's confessions to the Secret Police.

"Have you ever been to a ballet?" Bob asked as we approached the trailer.

I turned to look at him. "No, I've never been. Why?" I stopped breathing, sensing something wonderful was about to be said.

"If you'd like to go with me," Bob said, "meet me at the Bolshoi Theater tomorrow after your last show."

The Bolshoi was a two hundred-year-old institution that catered only to the finest of the performing arts. I've always known about the Bolshoi—I don't know how I knew, but I knew. "The Bolshoi?" I smiled, feeling dizzy just saying the name. "What time did you say?"

"I'll meet you in front of the Bolshoi at 7:45 p.m." Bob answered.

I looked back at Bob and played his voice again in my ear; it sounded so surreal. When I first heard the name Bolshoi, I never thought someone would one day say those words to me. But I had heard Bob clearly when he'd said, "I'll meet you in front of the Bolshoi at 7:45." How amazing!

Just before I disappeared inside the trailer, I shouted back at him, "Yes, you will! Not even a Russian revolution would stop me from meeting you at the Bolshoi tomorrow!" I heard Bob laugh.

The Bolshoi—that old, elegant name sounded lovely. For the occasion, I wanted to wear my most glamorous outfit. I had a black silk shantung dress designed and made by an FIT student who was an Italian American. I had a few classes with Tony; he was a good designer but also an excellent craftsman. I had seen students who were good designers, but their talent lay in pattern making. They could map out a garment like they were making a blueprint for the Taj Mughal. He was a great draftsman. But the dress he offered me had both elements—great design and great draftsmanship. So when he heard I was going to Russia, he offered to lend me the dress for the trip.

Since being in Russia, I had not worn it yet, as I wanted to keep it for a really special event—and the Bolshoi was special! I was flattered Tony was willing to let the dress out of his sight. It was a masterpiece, designed with sophisticated, clean lines. The bodice had a modest scoop neckline, a fitted waistband, and a knee-length fitted skirt, but the thrill of the dress was its sleeves that flared out like trumpets from the shoulders down to elbows.

I wore black pumps and carried a small black handbag. The dress was perfect for this special evening with Bob Robinson and the lavish Bolshoi Theater. I left the Leningradskya Hotel and took a taxi to the Bolshoi. A few minutes later, I found myself standing in front of the majestic Bolshoi Theatre. I looked at this magnificent building that fire had threatened to burn down several years ago.

I saw Bob, who stood tall and proud in front of the Bolshoi Theatre, waiting for me. He was dressed very elegantly, and I told him so, although compliments seemed to embarrass him. "Hi, Bob! Don't you look fetching this evening?" I jokingly teased him.

Not much for jokes, he replied by saying, "Madame, you are quite the picture yourself!"

I laughed, walked up to him, and took his arm, and together we entered the historic lobby. I felt all eyes look at us as we entered. Not only were we beautiful, but we were also two people of color, a double treat!

Bob had our tickets in hand, and he handed them to the usher, who then gave us our programs, and we were shown to our seats. Once seated, I looked around and whispered to Bob, "Ain't this just grand?"

Bob smiled. He had been raised in British schools in Jamaica, where English was always spoken properly. But he whispered with a satisfied look, "Indeed it 'tis!"

The theater lights slowly began to dim, and I was glad the pounding of my heart couldn't be heard. Fires had ravaged this amazing building on several occasions in the past. This building had been built before my great-grandparents, who narrowly escaped the devastating slave trade, were even born! So when the Bolshoi Theater opened its doors in 1756, a tradition of fine theatrical excellence was born. This was my very first ballet, thanks to my latest Russian friend, Bob Robinson, by way of Jamaica, British West Indies! How strange, surprising, and lovely life can be.

The Bolshoi Theater presented a ballet called "The Stone Flower, the Mistress of Copper Mount," a little-known ballet by Bazhov. I held my breath as the dancers silently floated out as quiet as butterflies. Their costumes were delicate shades of yellow and orange. I watch the dancers closely, knowing they were among the finest in the world. They moved with precision across the stage, their arms like wings, constantly fluttering up and down, simulating motion and flight. The full orchestra pleased our senses, making it possible for everyone to soar emotionally. The orchestra, with its many violins, commanding French horns, and shy oboes, sweetly lifted the dancers as they enraptured us in their skillful telling of the Bazhov saga.

Poor Stone Flower, encased in stone, waiting for her prince to come and rescue her. A pin, if dropped, could have been heard, as no one dared cough or sneeze. We sat all in rapt attention, carried away by the magic of Stone Flower's reawakening. She was once again gracefully dancing with her prince on that magical night and on that world-famous stage in the historical Bolshoi Theater!

When the heavy red velvet drapes finally fell, we in the audience jumped to our feet to release our tension through our grateful applause. We applauded until our arms were exhausted, knowing we had witnessed a great performance!

When we left the Bolshoi, I felt as if I were walking on air. I thanked Bob for an evening I would never forget. I think he was thrilled I so completely enjoyed spending this time with him enjoying an art he so enjoyed.

It was late, and we both had to work the next day. Bob escorted me to a taxi, where we said goodnight. My taxi took off in the direction of the Leningradskya, and I sat back and thought about this Brooklyn girl who had spent an evening in the world-famous Bolshoi Theater. I looked at the sky overhead, and tonight, it peacefully cradled twinkling stars. I was warmed by good friends and creative theater, and Moscow felt heavenly.

My friendship with Bob continued. He kept me engaged with stories of his time in Russia. I never tired of listening. Sometimes we met at

Sokolniki Park, but once (perhaps twice), I met him at his apartment. Bob's home was a neat one-bedroom flat that seemed to speak of the occupant and how he lived, hoping that on a moment's notice, he was being released—that a plane was waiting and he should not waste a second in grabbing his possessions and saying goodbye to the twenty-seven years he had lived in the Soviet Union.

It was in his apartment that Bob told me he had once been sent to Siberia on some job-related assignment. "Siberia? A man from tropical Jamaica? Were they crazy?" I asked Bob.

"I nearly died!" Bob said, shivering from the very thought of it. "I had never been so cold in my life! I ended up pleading with the company management to be returned to Moscow. The cold I experienced there was not fit for human beings—well, not those from tropical Jamaica!" Bob added. "I pleaded; if they didn't want to lose me as an employee, send me back to Moscow!"

"So, to this request, they listened and sent you back to Moscow, where it was not tropical, but degrees warmer than Siberia, which must sit on a lake of ice. Wow! Sounds pretty frightening. Siberia sounds unfriendly, distant, and isolated. I'm glad you were returned to Moscow, although Moscow is no picnic in the winter either!"

Bob laughed at my use of "no picnic" and said, "No, Moscow is definitely no picnic during the winter, but believe me, anyplace is better than Siberia!"

I believe Bob was happy in having someone to share his cultural journeys with, and I was happy to oblige.

Bob and I attended several concerts at Moscow's Tchaikovsky Concert Hall, where pictures of Lenin stared down from lofty places on the concert attendees. In all the years since Lenin's death, including the changes in Russia's leadership, Lenin was never replaced in the hearts of his people. His image was everywhere in Russia, and it seems Lenin was still the leader most Russians held dear.

We were in Tchaikovsky Hall, and it was great to hear Tchaikovsky's "Violin Concerto in D," "Piano Concerto No. 1," and "Pathetique" played in this hall named after him. He was a composer whose father wanted him to become a lawyer. Music lovers worldwide are glad Tchaikovsky disobeyed.

Through Bob, I met other African Americans living and thriving in Russia. One such person was a powerfully built man named George

W. Tynes who graduated from Wilberforce University in Ohio. He had traveled to Russia and was promised a life there without discrimination; on that promise, he become a Russian citizen. He married a woman from the Ukraine, and together they had three beautiful children of mixed hues. Mr. Tynes was the operator of a huge farm where he raised white ducks. On a pleasant day, we stood around a pond with what seemed like hundreds of ducks, plump and well-fed, swimming peacefully together. Mr. and Mrs. Tynes seemed devoted to each other. The father was of course bilingual, but his pleasant wife, who stayed by his side, spoke only Russian, as did their children. The family appeared to have an ideal life.

The youngest girl, who was nearly fifteen, stayed very close to me. She reminded me of a very pretty Eartha Kitt. I knew she had something she wanted to ask me, but she was waiting for a break in the conversation or to speak with me alone.

I decided to lag behind on the pretense of watching a family of ducks enter the pond. Quietly, she eased up to me and asked hesitantly if I could take her with me back to America. I was not expecting her question. I thought she might have wanted something I was wearing, like my bracelet or earrings. She spoke only a little English, so it was difficult to ask her the reason she wanted to leave her family and country. She obviously thought I could whisk her away from her parents by simply announcing I was taking her with me.

Regretfully, I had to tell her that to take her out of Russia, I would need her parents' consent. And that was not all; the red tape would be endless, and then like Bob Robinson, the government might refuse to let her go. She looked so disappointed that I felt I had personally let her down, but what she asked was an improbable task. I really wanted to know why she wished to leave her home, but she shied away, unable or unwilling to speak about it. I had only one theory that might not hold water, but in her school, she might have been taunted by white Russian children because of the color of her skin.

When Bob and I left, my heart went out to this girl who must have thought she'd be walking out with us.

Bob Ross was another acquaintance of Bob Robinson's. Ross, who had twice married and divorced Russian women, was a transplanted African American who now made his home in Moscow. He was used as a propaganda agent for the Communist Party and was paid quite well to spread his disparaging remarks about how America treats its African

American population. Bob Ross conducted seminars on this topic, although his last visit to America had been thirty years ago. But in the end, Bob Ross's only value to Russia was in spreading negative Communist Party propaganda against the United States. If the Soviet government's focus ever changed from the speeches Ross made to another attention-grabbing issue, then Bob Ross might find himself out of a job, his luxury apartment, and his expensive car.

Bob Robinson remained in Moscow another seventeen years after I left, a total of forty-four years. Twenty years later, as I dressed while at home in Brooklyn, the television was on, and I heard Bryant Gumbel, the host of the *Today Show,* say, "I understand you still look over your shoulder even today!"

Still not looking at the TV screen, I then heard a voice that was strangely familiar respond, "Yes, because Russia is a very vindictive country!" I ran back in the room to see the face, knowing it could be none other than Bob Robinson! I was too late, but Bryant Gumbel was holding up a book entitled *Black on Red, My Forty-Four Years in the Soviet Union.*

I smiled. Bob had gotten out and written about his experiences. I called NBC, hoping to speak with Bob, but they gave me his publisher's number instead. I then called the publisher and left my name and phone number. Two weeks later, Bob called. I couldn't believe I was talking to my old friend again, and we arranged to meet.

I met Bob at Union Station in Washington. As I stepped from the train onto the platform, Bob was waiting! I marveled at how fate had brought us together again.

He was older, and so was I. He insisted on carrying my suitcase. I tried to refuse him, saying it wasn't heavy, but Bob was Bob, and I knew from years ago that when he set his mind to something, it was useless to try and talk him out of it. I handed over my suitcase, and we found a restaurant in Union Station to sit and talk. "How did you do it, Bob? How did you get out of Russia?" I couldn't wait to ask that question.

"I never gave up!" Bob said. "Every angle that presented itself, I tried. I failed time and time again. But one night, at a social gathering at the Russian Embassy, I saw Idi Amin. Idi Amin was one of Russia's favorite African sons! I walked up to him and told him how long I'd been in Russia but that my dream was to go to Uganda to teach. I simply asked if he could help me get to Uganda."

"And did he?"

"One month later, I was packing to leave for Uganda!" Bob said triumphantly. "But just as I was getting ready to board the plane, I was stopped."

"Stopped? Why?"

"That's what I wanted to know! I was angry! She said I needed to be vaccinated!"

"How thoughtful," I said, being facetious.

"I told her I had already been vaccinated. She said I'd been given the wrong vaccination. I didn't believe her. I missed my flight."

"Oh, no—but eventually, you made it. You made it to Uganda."

"Yes. They couldn't find anything else to hold me back, so I finally did get to Uganda, and I taught there for seven years!"

"And you got married, I heard."

Bob looked happy. I remembered him telling me he would never marry a Russian woman, and he had not. "Yes, I married a beautiful African American who had been teaching in Uganda." After getting married, Bob and his bride left Uganda, and Bob finally made it to the United States.

We were now both in Washington. I looked at this man who sat before me, and it seemed he had lived several lifetimes in one. Just thinking of the history he had lived through during his forty-four years in Russia was staggering. He had lived there through the dictatorships of Stalin, Brezhnev, Khrushchev, and Malenkov. But he had survived, and here he was, sitting across from me, casually having a cup of tea. He was older now but still slim and fit. He had carried my bags just as though he was the man I met all those years ago in Moscow.

I know twenty years ago, Bob was younger than he was that day as we sat sipping tea in Union Station, but he was a happier man than he was when he was in Russia. As a result, he was younger in spirit, which gave him a youthfulness that belied his years. He had finished his memoirs about his forty-four years in Russia.

Bob was looking for a screenwriter, because he wanted his experiences in Russia to become a motion picture. He had already decided he wanted movie star Denzel Washington to play the leading role! He was happy to be back in the United States with his bride. I now know all those plans, hopes, and expectations kept him going. I could hardly believe it when he told me he was eighty years young!

Robert Robinson a resident of Russia for forty four years,
and I in Washington, DC

CHAPTER 17

Boris and Tamara

As a model for the fashion show at the American National Exhibition in Moscow, every day was an adventure and presented me with an opportunity to meet someone interesting and new. At nearly all of the fashion shows, we had record crowds of up to four thousand Russians. At the end of each show was the feeling of goodwill as the audience applauded us and we Americans applauded the audience in return.

As the days moved into mid-August, there was an approaching chill in the air. But our show continued to attract thousands, and one night, after the last show for the day was over, an attractive Russian couple greeted me when I stepped out of the trailer.

She was an attractive, petite Russian girl with short, light brown hair, soft hazel eyes, a ready smile, and as they say in the States, a peaches-and-cream complexion. He was blond and very handsome and had a charming shyness about him.

They introduced themselves as Boris and Tamara, and they were students at an art school in Moscow. We spent some time talking and getting to know each other, and there seemed to be a rapport between us. As it was after 8:00, I was asked to join them for dinner. With no other plans for the evening, I accepted. We walked over to the Praga Restaurant, where I had dined before. I learned Tamara was twenty-six and divorced. At one time, she and Boris had been an item, but now they were simply friends.

Although I was taller than Tamara, we were the exact same dress size. I would learn she had a passion for Western clothes, and we eventually struck up a deal; Tamara wanted to buy any of my personal wardrobe I'd be willing to sell her. She defended her love for American-made clothes by explaining that Russian-made clothes tended to desexualize the female figure—and she was right. Russia was an industrial country, and fashion came almost as an afterthought. I had no problem with her buying the clothes I'd brought, because in doing so, she would free up space in my suitcase for the souvenirs I'd take home. I knew when I returned home, I could buy more clothes, but Tamara did not have the luxury of shopping at a Macy's, Bergdorf Goodman, or Saks. Whatever I wore when we would meet, Tamara loved. Although I would offer her an item or two, she would never accept gifts. She always insisted on paying for the clothes she liked and saw me wear.

While dining at the Praga Restaurant one night, Tamara and Boris made me an offer I thought was so fantastic, I couldn't refuse. "We want to paint your portrait," she said as Boris looked on eagerly. "We would like to take painted portraits of you to school with us in September."

"Yes," Boris said, "eight."

"Eight portraits?" I asked, wondering how long it would take them to paint eight portraits. The American National Exhibition in Moscow would be closing in three weeks. Would they have enough time?

"Yes," Boris continued, "we will paint four each of you." He produced his disarming smile as he added, "And for your time, two portraits for you."

Wow, how nice. I'd get two self-portraits painted by two Russian artists. Their proposition seemed like a win-win situation. But just when I was warming up to the idea, I wondered where this painting could take place. Not in my hotel room—it was against the law. Bringing Americans to their homes was avoided by Russians for fear family or neighborhood spies might report them to the KGB.

Finally, I said, as they sat waiting for my decision, "I love the idea!" They both smiled. "But where? Are you going to paint on a park bench?"

For a second, no one spoke, and then Tamara said, "I have a studio."

"You do? That's marvelous!" I said, knowing spaces were at a premium in Moscow, and to maintain an apartment and a studio as well was a costly affair. But I knew better than to question a Russian in front of another Russian, so I simply smiled, knowing a studio was the perfect solution.

Tamara wrote on a piece of paper the name of the street where she would be waiting for me at 9:00 the next morning. They would paint until noon, and Boris would escort me to Sokolniki Park so I could prepare for the 2:00 fashion show. We would meet four mornings a week. I'd leave the Leningradskya Hotel and take a taxi to the corner where Tamara would be waiting. So that I would be inconspicuous, I was to wear clothes in dark colors, browns and grays, nothing in bright shades that would attract attention. Heaven knows, even though there was nothing wrong with what we wanted to do, I didn't want the KGB in on the project.

After paying the taxi driver, I stepped out of the cab. As the cab drove off, Tamara emerged from around a corner. We said a quick hello, hurried down the street together, and entered a huge courtyard of a well-maintained limestone building. The building was built like a fortress with several doors leading into a spacious lobby.

The lobby had at least four stairwells to different sections of the building. Tamara and I ran up a flight of stairs to the second floor. I watched as Tamara inserted a key into a huge door and it sprang open. She stepped in and beckoned me to follow. Tamara hastily closed and locked the door. We were in a small hall room, and while I stood there, she dashed over to the only window in the room, the one window from which bright sunshine poured in. This was sunshine an artist would use to paint a subject. She pulled the window shade down. Immediately, the room darkened. I must have looked surprised, because she explained while looking embarrassed, "My neighbors are snoops. If they can see in my room, they might report what they see to the KGB."

"I understand," I said simply as I sat on her daybed, the only place there was to sit.

An electrical cord hung from the ceiling from which dangled a small light bulb. Tamara clicked on the switch, and the small light bulb lit up. Although the light it provided was no match for the natural sunlight, for the artists, it would have to do.

A wooden credenza sat opposite the daybed. On it, Tamara had a bunch of tiny grapes in a glass bowl, and next to the bowl was a small transistor radio. "I listen to news from the Russian press, but I also listen to Radio Free Europe—which is forbidden, of course, but what can I do? I don't always trust the Russian press to report the news accurately."

I helped myself to a few of the grapes as she talked. I knew to have Radio Free Europe was another criminal offense. But I knew many Russians listened to world news on Radio Free Europe, not always trusting Russian news casts.

Tamara quickly reached under her daybed, pulled out a secret stack of canvases, and placed them on the bed. I looked at them and realized they were stacks of abstract paintings, another criminal offense—not only, but also to own. "You painted these?" She nodded with a smile. "I really like them. Your sense of color is really strong, and so is your sense of composition and form. I think they reflect your bold personality. You're really good!"

Tamara said little but was obviously pleased to have an audience for her work. In showing me her works, she also revealed the trust she had in me to keep her secret. In a few minutes, she placed them back under the daybed just in time to hear a gentle tap on the door. We knew it was Boris. Tamara opened the door, and Boris entered, bringing his art supplies and sunny disposition. I knew better than to mention even to Boris Tamar's collection of abstract art. I wouldn't want word of her affection for that art form to get out because the government was intolerant of anyone who disobeyed their decree against it. Offenders (and she was one) were sent away to prison for many years. Once their easels were set up, I assumed the pose we agreed on, and they began to paint.

At noon, we left the studio. Tamara was off to another appointment while Boris and I strolled the tree-lined streets leading to Sokolniki Park. Because Boris was very easygoing, we got along well.

One day, after the painting session, Boris and I walked past a small pond that happened to have three swans in it. The setting looked for all the world like a painting.

Boris became excited, pointed, and said "Look!" I looked, and he said something to the effect that the scene was like in my ballet! I looked again and realized what he meant by my ballet. It was true that the scene before us could have been an ad for the ballet *Swan Lake*. I laughed, reminding him it wasn't my ballet but his, since it was written by Tchaikovsky.

We watched them for a few minutes. Then Boris took my arm, and we walked on, arriving at Sokolniki Park in time for me to dress and appear on stage. At the park entrance, I would leave him, saying, "See you tomorrow." But today was my day off, and Tamara suggested Boris take me to visit GUMS department store.

It was a cold day. As we neared mid-August, temperatures had dipped. My summer clothing and spring coats now needed to be layered to achieve any warmth. Suddenly, few places in Moscow felt warm. We Americans discovered that the heating system was controlled by the state, and the heat was turned off from mid-April to mid-October. When the weather was consistently in the eighties, their no-heat policy worked fine, but when the weather turned frigid, it made for much discomfort.

GUMS, which stood for State Universal Store and was pronounced "gooms," was located on the eastern side of Red Square. It was Catherine ll who commissioned an Italian architect, Giaromo Quarenghi, to design and complete the structure in 1912. GUMS was several stories high, and inside there were arched alcoves where vendors displayed merchandise for sale. Glass domes covered the entire structure, which was strong enough to support accumulations of snow during Moscow's severe winters. Once you were inside, it was said the entire structure resembled an English train station. I couldn't wait to see it.

Boris hailed a taxi, and we climbed in. I was really cold, so I sat close to Boris, hoping to soak up some of his warmth. While talking, Boris strategically placed his ungloved hand on my bare knee. There was something very sensual in that touch. I was so affected that hot shivers ran through me, replacing the numbing chill I felt only seconds ago. Sensing my reaction to his touch, he turned my face to his and kissed me. I yielded. As our lips touched, I wondered if he had always felt this way toward me. Since our first meeting, we had spent much time together, and he never displayed any indication of this hot passion.

As the cab sped through the streets, we kissed again and again, relishing each other and each kiss, wanting to remember the sweetness of the moment. I knew if given time, I could fall for this gentle Russian who made my heart whisper his name. But his name was not what I heard next. The Russian word "Nyet" broke into our bliss. "Nyet, nyet!" the taxi driver screamed while adding a loud rapping sound as he banged on the inside glass window of the taxi. Boris bolted straight up! I did too. The taxi driver was screaming at us. I was concerned for him, as his face turned a crimson red. Although I didn't understand all he was shouting, I knew he was scolding us, forbidding us our kisses in his cab.

If I hadn't been so embarrassed, I might have found the situation humorous. But we both removed our arms from around each other. Boris instead took my hand, securing me next to him until the tirade from the driver was over. We sat, casting our eyes downward, feeling like children caught stealing cookies from a cookie jar. For the remainder of the trip, we dared not look at each other, fearing the urge to kiss again would be too strong to resist. But as the taxi wheels rumbled over the cobblestone streets, we could feel the driver monitoring us through his rear view mirror, his eyes staring at us disapprovingly. I wondered what he disapproved of most—a black girl and a Russian boy displaying affection? Or did he think during that short trip we might procreate like rabbits, thus exiting his cab leaving a dozen or so bunnies in his care? When our taxi arrived at GUMS, we got out and watched as the angry driver sped away. I turned and looked at the building of GUMS department store. It was unlike any building I had ever seen. Boris smiled as he linked his arm in mine, happy with my reaction to seeing this national treasure.

Inside this trapezoidal building with its steel frame and glass roof, who wouldn't have been impressed? At one time, GUMS had 1,200 vendors, but today, approximately two hundred are found there. Joseph Stalin had closed GUMS down for several years, and it became his headquarters for a while. Then GUMS was where Stalin allowed his wife's body to lie in state after her suicide. But later GUMS became a mall again. Boris and I roamed its halls, arm in arm, checking out the vendors. We found a balalaika, a kind of Russian banjo. I ended up buying it plus some black lacquer Russian boxes and a few stackable Russian dolls as gifts to take home.

Time spent in GUMS had been lovely, but nothing compared to the passion Boris and I had shared earlier! From GUMS, we walked to the Praga, where we met Tamara and had dinner.

The painting sessions continued until all eight portraits were done. Tamara's style of painting was more naturalistic, whereas Boris' style was more stylized.

In Tamara's tiny room, all eight oil paintings were spread out before me. It was strange looking at eight likenesses of myself; yet Boris and Tamara had managed to make them all look different. "Chose one painting from each of us," Boris instructed.

I looked each painting over. "It's difficult; they're all so good!"

In Boris's painting, I looked like a Madonna, and my image had an attitude of aloofness and piety. He rendered my red and white checkered shirt as a solid red. In Tamara's painting, I appeared like the girl next door, happy and youthful. Each artist had rendered an interesting perspective of me.

Finally, I dived in and selected the two paintings I would own. They were large, eighteen by twenty-seven inches in size. This whole painting venture had been well worth it. I had two oil portraits, definitely ensuring I would always remember my friendship with two wonderful artists! "Your instructor should give you all As," I said, and Boris and Tamara laughed. "I will treasure these portraits," I added, feeling emotional, "and the memories of our time together."

We felt quite happy as we stood in that tiny hall room, pleased at having seen our project through to its completion.

Does life imitate art, or is it the other way around? Gil Noble and Norma Jean Johnston were African American models in the fashion show. They were also engaged to be married. Norma Jean was a pretty, brown-skinned woman with a ready smile whose profession was that of a nurse. Gil was a handsome man who later became the host of a television show in New York called *Like It Is*. He was also a gifted pianist. Gil was six foot five, and in Moscow, he could be seen from two blocks away because he towered over Russian men who tended to be well under six feet.

If only those 240 troublesome ladies of the press could have been at the US Embassy in Moscow months later for Gil and Norma's wedding. Both bride and groom hailed from Jamaica, and they had a white couple as their attendants in their wedding. The bride wore a lovely white gown and veil; the groom was in a black tux. The wedding contradicted the ladies of the press, who said such a wedding—a black bride and groom and a white couple in attendance—would never happen. But sorry, ladies; it did!

One of my portraits painted by a Russian artist in Moscow

CHAPTER 18

An Ousted Art Form

Years ago, the Hermitage Museum was located in St. Petersburg and had thousands of works of art by artists from around the world. But in 1918, when Moscow became Russia's capitol, the art from the Hermitage was transferred to the Pushkin Museum.

I was grateful when Boris and Tamara invited me to visit the museum with them. One afternoon, I met them in front of the Pushkin/Hermitage building. The solid structure of the building spoke of the importance of the collection of art inside. It was a massive light gray stone building that was built like a fortress.

Boris held the door open, and Tamara and I stepped inside. Immediately, I sensed a silent reverence for the collection inside. We faced an interior of gleaming marble floors in halls and corridors supported by Ionic and Doric marble columns that stood boldly tall and majestically elegant, gracing the ornately decorated ceilings. Elaborately flocked paper adorned the walls while wingback chairs made of silk brocaded fabrics stood in corners, not to be used as chairs but simply to be admired.

There were also larger-than-life sized statues, each magnificently carved in marble and appearing frozen in time but involved in some activity like catching a moon beam or contemplating a frog in a pond. They crouched unaware of their physical perfection. Everywhere we looked, there was a distinct feeling of going back in time to an era rich in history and opulence.

As we moved from room to room, from exhibit to exhibit, our eyes drank in the enormous compilation of priceless ancient Egyptian, Greek, and Western European art. There was also a major trove of art from masters like Van Gogh, Gauguin, Picasso, and Matisse, to name a few. Who would have thought so much of the world's great artists could all be found in one country under one roof?

We found ourselves in a room in which all four walls were covered with original works by Vincent van Gogh. To see one or two original works by the Dutch artist would have been remarkable, but to enter a room in which in neat order, all four walls housed canvas after canvas of works by this artist was stunning! All those canvases with blazingly intense pigments from Van Gogh's profuse use of red, orange, and yellow hues actually gave the room the feeling of heat.

We walked into the adjoining room, which had a huge collection of paintings by French artists such as Monet. Then in the next room was Manet; both had a large representation of their work on the walls. The sheer number of canvases on which they used cooler tones of blues, grays, and light purples actually seemed to lower the temperature in the room. I was amazed at how our brains were affected by color.

To say it was a thrilling experience to see such a huge collection of art all under one roof would certainly be an understatement. Russia's involvement in various political conflicts in which Russia confiscated works of art has not been disputed. But most of the credit for Russia's love affair with art can be credited to Catherine the Great, who in 1764 began collecting art on a massive scale for her palace in Saint Petersburg. Her appetite for art from various nations was inexhaustible, and her pocketbook contained the money necessary to handsomely reward the seller!

Tamara, who acted as our tour guide, was most knowledgeable about the museum in general. She led us through all the exhibits; then after we'd been in the museum for several hours, she led us to a room that was off-limits to all tourists. I wondered how she even knew of this room, but in thinking back at how she led us from exhibit to exhibit in such a methodical way, I knew she had spent an inordinate amount of time here. I was grateful for her knowledge of this amazing place and grateful she wanted to share it with us.

Boris, being an art student, must have visited here often. But I never knew what Boris knew because he never in any way gave himself away. He had introduced himself as Boris and said that he was an art student, but all else was a mystery. Because he kept everything to himself, he seemed like the kind of guy you could reveal your most heinous secret to, and he would never tell a soul. Besides being handsome, this ability to just blend in was one of his charms. He was always there but never obtrusive.

Later, Tamara took us to a very isolated section of the museum, and there we entered a hallway that led to an enormous but dimly lit room. Once our eyes adjusted, and there was no need for her to take us in because from the doorway, we could look in on the haphazard way the art was kept. Carelessly strewn canvases of abstract paintings lay discarded on the floor. The paintings had been piled high, one on top of the other, accumulating dust from years of isolation and neglect. I was willing to bet that on the floor of this room lay works from world-famous artists whose work sold in the hundreds of thousands of dollars but were now discarded, never to see the light of day again.

The Russian government had declared an all-out war against abstract art. If an artist openly created such art, that artist would be arrested for what amounted to committing a crime against the state. So as Tamara, Boris, and I stood in this desolate storage room, I sensed that Tamara, an abstract artist herself, mourned the slow death the Soviet government had imposed on this art form. This room was the end of the line for these canvases, but at least they had not been destroyed. Hopefully, the abstract art these canvases contained might languish here until perhaps one day their death sentence might be commuted.

It seemed a curious stance for a government to take, but like their stance against religion, perhaps abstract art indicated a kind of free thinking on the part of the individual. Perhaps a free thinker was a danger to this government. Perhaps the Soviet Union found that abstract art somehow filled a void left behind by the forced separation from religion. Whatever the reason, painting or owning such paintings could mean spending many years in a Russian prison.

CHAPTER 19

Mixed Racial Messages

I went shopping one day for a few items in a small grocery store in Moscow. The store was busy with shoppers who stood in a line to pay for their purchases, and I followed suit. After having paid for my items—some cookies, tea, and sugar—I went outside to where, if I waited in line, I would eventually get a taxi. A light rain fell, but I found my place in the line behind approximately eight or nine others who also wanted a taxi. I knew those in line were anxious to get home, as I realized many had worked that day, and some were elderly. When a taxi finally did pull up, all the women in front of and behind me, as though from a previous discussion, insisted I take the cab. "No, no, but thank you. I can wait my turn," I said, feeling okay about waiting.

But the ladies would not take no for an answer. They insisted on my taking the taxi. "No, no. nyet, nyet!" I said again, but they insisted.

I realized I graciously had to accept the taxi. So I made my way past those who stood in line before me. Somehow this didn't seem right or fair, but I smiled and thanked them as I climbed into the cab. As the taxi pulled off, I looked back at the women as they stood in line in the rain. I was puzzled. Why did they insist on me taking the cab? Was it a kindness they extended to any visitor? Would they have extended this same kindness to a twenty-one-year-old white female visitor? Or was it a kindness they extended to black visitors?

I wondered if they felt obligated to treat me special because they heard the plight blacks had suffered in the United States and somehow wanted to make up for it by being kind to me. This incident reminded me of Goldie and a talk she and I had had in her apartment in Moscow a few weeks ago. Goldie was a biracial Afro-Russian woman born in Russia. Goldie's parents, an African American man and a Jewish woman, fell in love in United States back in the 1920s. But the United States was not accepting of interracial couples, and most states banned interracial marriages.

After much discussion, it was decided that they would migrate to Russia, believing Russian society would be tolerant of their relationship. But even in Russia, they still had their hurdles. At least they were able to live together and not fear for their lives. Two years later, their only child, Goldie, was born on Russian soil, and she was a light tan-colored Russian citizen.

She attended schools in the neighborhood at which she received a thorough Russian education. Upon graduation, Goldie began working, and while working, she met a young Russian fellow. It was love at first sight for both, and marriage quickly followed. The groom's family who saw this relationship unfold secretly didn't want this marriage for him. Little by little, they began chipping away at this love match, wanting to find its breaking point. They applied pressure on the young man to abandon his marriage and divorce his wife. "She is not one of us."

"But she is a Russian," he said.

"No, not really," they said.

He became distraught, and in total despair, he ended his life as he jumped from the subway platform into the path of an oncoming subway train. It took years for Goldie to get over his death and the reasons that had led to it.

It was apparent to me that racial conflict was alive and well on several levels in Russia. It also seemed apparent that in most of Russian society, when the subject of interracial relationships hit home and affected Russian's personally, similar racial attitudes surfaced.

After telling her story, Goldie, asked if I could make her appear like an American. When I asked her why appearing like an American was important; her answer was, "If Russians think I am an American or a visitor to Russia, they tended to treat me better or somehow differently than if they know I am a Russian native."

Goldie wanted my American-made shoes, and of course, any clothes I brought that could transform her. My wardrobe was slowly dwindling because of Russian women who wanted clothes made in America.

But hopefully whatever clothes I had left in my suitcase would make Goldie appear foreign to her fellow Russians. Her attempts to make herself over were merely a Band-Aid on a much larger problem—the treatment or lack of regard she felt because she was of mixed race.

Although Russian women tended not to wear makeup, Goldie asked me to give her lipstick and mascara, and I was glad I had brought extras. She also wanted her curly brown hair straightened, and I straightened it. I did what I could, and when I was finished, I looked at the new Goldie and liked what I saw. She looked great! But how long could this makeover last? Where would she get more westernized clothes, shoes, makeup, or someone to style her hair? These things were just not available to her in Moscow.

She was a true citizen of Russia; she had been born there. How long would she have to pretend being someone else, especially passing as a foreigner, to be treated with a higher regard in this the country of her birth? I concluded that Russian society was at best a complex society when it came to race relations, and for those of color who lived there, there was a balancing act on a tightrope that had to be carefully navigated.

I have read that when singer, athlete, actor, and activist Paul Robeson visited Russia and saw the maze of racial ambiguity, he left disillusioned.

CHAPTER 20

Difficult in Any Language

It was early September, and we Americans had only a few more days left in Moscow. For several weeks, the warm weather had become a thing of the past, and a merciless winter was already ushering in low temperatures accompanied by snow and icy rain.

As was the tradition, heat to State-owned businesses was turned off from mid-April to mid-October. So if cold weather arrived early—late August or early September—October was a long way off. But the State never relented. Having the State reinstate heat during an early winter never happened. Hotels, theaters, restaurants, etc. were owned by the State.

My body adjusted poorly to living in a room that had the look of warmth (carpets on the floor, drapes on the windows, comfortable couches, and soft blankets on the bed) but was no warmer than outside. As a result, I suffered from the worst cold I'd ever had in my life. My head ached, my nose ran, my throat was scratchy, and on top of it all, I was also suffering severe stomach cramps. I admit, I was a mess.

I felt achy from head to toe. Even my eyes hurt, and I knew if we didn't soon leave Moscow, I'd end up with another Russian memory of a visit to a local hospital in Moscow. I was in my hotel bed, lying under layers of blankets, feeling sorry that the Russian winter had snapped all my get-up-and-go.

My bedside phone suddenly rang, a shrill sound that jolted me. I inched my hand out from beneath the covers to answer it. "Hello?" I said. The voice was unfamiliar to me. "Who is this?" I asked, and he explained, making me recall him. "Oh, yes. Of course I remember you. Yes, I saw you a few nights ago at the Praga."

It was Giorgi, a young Russian I and a few other Americans had dined with at the Praga perhaps twice in the last two weeks. I couldn't figure out why he was calling me or where he was calling from. There was no way he could be in the lobby; Russians could be arrested for even being in the lobby of hotels where Americans stayed. "Jackie," he said (it came out sounding like "Jocky"), "please come outside with me." I noted the sound of urgency in his voice. He said the one phrase that made me recoil: "Come outside!" Anything that had to do with the outside had no allure for me.

"Giorgi," I said patiently and slowly to make sure he understood, "I feel miserable. I have a very, very bad cold. It is raining and cold outside, and even my hotel room is frigid because the hotel has no heat, so I really have no plans to go anywhere this morning."

"I have something to tell you," he insisted, like he had not heard a word I'd said.

"Really? What is it?" I asked, wanting him to tell me over the phone.

"It is very difficult to say in English and very difficult to say in Russian," he explained. "Please meet me in front of your hotel."

"But, Giorgi …"

"Please, I have something very important to tell you." Important? What could Giorgi have to tell me? Why wouldn't he tell me over the phone? "Please," I heard him practically begging. "I must tell you something."

I relented. "Give me a few minutes to get dressed," I said. "I'll meet you in front of the hotel."

I hung up the phone, angry with myself for agreeing to meet him and annoyed that I was dragging my sick body out of my cold hotel room and outside into the frigid icy morning rain. But I was curious as to what Giorgi felt was so urgent, and as he had said, difficult to say in English and Russian. I was intrigued, and sick or not, my curiosity got the better of me.

I remembered Giorgi as being reserved but friendly. If we spoke at all, we'd said no more than "Hello." As I dressed, I thought about what he had just said. It would be interesting to know what he felt was so urgent and difficult to speak about in Russian or English.

I dressed in layers, hoping to hold on to my body heat. I put on a long-sleeved dress; the only coat I had, a lightweight wool spring coat; and a scarf I wrapped over my head and around my neck. I had no boots, so slipped on a pair of socks and my brown leather flats. I took the elevator down to the lobby and walked out the front door. I saw Giorgi immediately; he was standing across the street, wearing a black raincoat and holding a black umbrella. I had been annoyed with him, but as I looked at him standing in the icy rain, I knew he had to be freezing. I wondered again what was so important that he would come out on a day like today.

"Hi, Giorgi," I said as I joined him under his umbrella. Like a winter coat, I had not brought boots or an umbrella to Moscow.

Giorgi said, "Hello," and although I was the one with the miserable cold, Giorgi looked more miserable than I. He was a nice-looking guy, I noted, with black curly hair, gray eyes, and the high cheek bones I'd found in many Russians who might have had a mixture of Asian blood. Giorgi immediately began to walk; his feet must have been freezing. I walked beside him. My light wool coat suddenly felt paper-thin, and I shivered as I looped my arm into his so that we might keep warm and both fit under his umbrella.

"What do you have to tell me?" I looked at him, waiting for him to speak.

"It is difficult to say in English and difficult to say in Russian," he repeated again, looking hopeless.

"What could be so difficult, Giorgi?" I asked, looking down, trying to avoid the puddles.

Glancing up, Giorgi wore an expression of pure agony.

"Won't you tell me?" I asked him.

We walked on in silence, and at the corner, we turned right and continued walking down the rain-soaked sidewalk. The day was gray, and I wanted some sunshine, but there was none. At the next corner, we again turned right and walked around the block. We circled the block twice more. Giorgi seemed oblivious of the freezing rain. Well, why shouldn't he? He was Russian and conditioned to this extreme weather. After three trips around the block, my clothes were wet, and my shoes squeaked and oozed water with each step. I thought how good it would be to find a warm place to just sit, but no such place seemed to exist until October, and this was only early September. I chided myself for such foolish thoughts and turned to Giorgi. "Giorgi, you've got to tell me something, anything! We have walked around the block three times, and honestly, I don't look forward to making that trip again!"

"It is very difficult …" Giorgi began.

"What is?"

"It is difficult to say it in English, and it is—"

"I know, I know; it's difficult to say it in Russian." I finished his sentence for him and asked with exasperation, "What could be so difficult?"

Finally, the expression on Giorgi's face cleared. He looked like a child who had refused to take a bitter-tasting medicine but was relenting, finding the courage to swallow it all. I remained silent, afraid if I spoke, I might affect the resolve I saw on his face. Hopefully he was about to say whatever was causing him such anxiety. I waited, but I silently swore that if he said anything about it being difficult to say in English or Russian, I was marching back into the hotel and up to my cold but waiting bed.

As we stood and stared at each other, Giorgi finally spoke, and I couldn't believe he was saying those words again! "It is very difficult to say in English and difficult to say in Russian," he started, and before I could interrupt him, he finally ended by saying, "I love you."

I stood back in shock, forgoing my space under his umbrella, letting the rain run down my face. I had not expected what he had just said. I thought, *Oh, these crazy Russians* and gave an affectionate chuckle. But that would not be appropriate today, because Giorgi was serious. Until today, he and I had not even stood this close before. I was flattered, but Giorgi could not be serious—could he? We'd met twice; did he believe in love at first sight? Did I? It was out and had been said—this thing that was difficult to say in English and Russian. He was right. To tell someone you loved them, not knowing how it would be received, was certainly difficult in any language!

Now for the first time, I noticed his gray eyes that had a touch of hazel; I looked at the blush on his cheeks and wondered if it was because of what he'd just said or the result of the frigid chill in the air. But why had he chosen to tell me his feelings today? Surely he knew I'd be leaving Moscow in a few days, and most likely, the two of us would never meet again. But then another thought entered my head; perhaps it was not about romance at all. Perhaps his veiled notion was that a relationship with an American might lead to an opportunity to exit Russia and come to America. Either way, who was Giorgi? There was not even time to find out. "Giorgi," I said softly, "once I'm home, I'll write to you, and hopefully, one day you can visit America. Wouldn't you like that?"

His eyes seemed to shine as I spoke about the possibility of him visiting the United States. I then leaned forward and kissed him softly on his cheek. In doing so, I realized watching Russians disapproved of public displays of affection.

But Giorgi did not shy away from my kiss or try to stop me when I whispered, "Goodbye, Giorgi." I turned and walked across the street and into the lobby of the Leningradskya Hotel. When I glanced back, Giorgi was slowly walking down the street, holding his umbrella, as the icy rain continued to fall.

CHAPTER 21

Too Sick for Romance

After leaving Giorgi, I returned to my room and climbed back into bed—not seeking warmth, because there was none, but just wanting to lie down. I lay there, shivering, waiting for the heat from my body to warm my bed. I felt worse than I had earlier, and I realized being out in the freezing rain for nearly two hours with Giorgi had not been wise. So as I lay in bed with a runny nose, sore throat, weepy eyes, and severe cramps, I felt totally useless and unfit to live with. I drifted off to sleep. A few hours later, the phone on my table suddenly rang.

Who could be calling? Was it Giorgi again? I answered, and although his words were rushed, I recognized Boris's voice! He spoke quickly, but I understood enough to know he was in the hotel and on his way to my room! *Oh, no, not Boris!* I was immediately concerned about him. Surely he knew he could be arrested just for being in the hotel. I knew Boris knew the danger he was putting himself in, and I worried about him taking such a chance—especially today, of all days, when I felt so awful and it was so cold. How I wished I looked pretty and could greet him at the door. I wanted to open that door and invite him into a warm space. I simply wished I felt up to entertaining him, making the risk he was taking worthwhile. I never wanted Boris to see me sneezing and coughing or feeling miserable, but there was no way to avoid it; he was in the hotel and heading to my room!

I heard the light tap on the door, and I called for him to come in. When he entered and I saw him, I really wanted to feel better and feel pretty. But I couldn't even pretend that my nose wasn't stuffy, my eyes weren't watery, and my cough wasn't deep like that of a frog. I was miserable, and Boris was out of breath from the rushing and the anxiety.

I lay flat on my back, looking at my blond Adonis who stood at the foot of my bed.

I could tell he wasn't sure what his next move should be. I had a sneezing fit—one sneeze after the other (brought on, I'm sure, by the anxiety I felt). We both felt anxious. I doubted Boris had ever put himself in a situation like this before, risking arrest to be with a woman. If I had not felt so bad, I would have been flattered. I knew he came knowing this might be our only chance to be together. But I didn't seem to have the strength to rise; each cough and abdominal cramp seemed to weaken me. I wanted a hot bath, but there was no hot water. Even as Boris stood there, I could see his breath; that's how frigid the air was inside my room. To see someone's breath while they were inside a room was crazy!

This day was like a comedy of errors. To remove my blankets would have been akin to walking naked in the streets. Suddenly, without removing his jacket, Boris dived onto the bed. The excitement of it must have been too much for me, because I had coughing spasms. I excused myself as I reached past him for a clean cloth on the night table, and I proceeded to wipe my weepy eyes and runny nose and then repeat the coughing and wheezing again. Instead of wanting to cuddle, I wanted to ball up in a fetal position. But nevertheless, Boris began trying to rush things between us while I muffled more sneezes and wished my stomach cramps would go away.

Fully dressed, Boris was soon under my blankets, and although perhaps he didn't understand what I was saying, he eventually began to comprehend that the time for this romantic escapade was unfortunately not now. If life events were dictated by the alignment of the stars, then on this day, the stars were sadly misaligned. Boris must have understood at last how awful I felt. He regained his composure and climbed out of the bed. I had mixed emotions as I lay looking at him; I wanted him to stay but I knew he could not. I could not have avoided getting sick with this hotel being minus any heat at all. My cramps were an unavoidable part of my history, but I had learned to live with them—although never combined with these frigid conditions.

Boris stood at the side of my bed and offered me a weak smile. I apologized with my eyes. As quickly as he had come, he was gone.

Perhaps, I thought later, if there had been a plan and not this surprise visit, and if he had not felt under pressure to be in and out of the hotel before being discovered, if my room had not been as cold as Siberia and Boris had been able to secure hot blankets and towels to wrap me in ... The what ifs seemed endless, and I thought *Perhaps this ... but then perhaps that* ... But then I concluded that perhaps none of it was supposed to happen.

After a shopping trip to GUMS Department Store,
Boris and I pose

CHAPTER 22

Hard to Say Goodbye

We Americans were leaving Russia, and Tamara and Boris asked if they could accompany me to the airport. I believed they wanted to be there because our friendship mattered. Tamara had taken me into her confidence in several ways. She revealed her abstract collection to me when she was unable to trust even her family, so it was clear that she found someone she could trust. I have since wondered about a nation that could feel threatened by an art form.

On another occasion, when I visited her studio and we were alone for a few minutes before Boris was to arrive, she spoke about her grandmother. As tears fell, Tamara told me her grandmother, whom she loved, believed if there was ever a war between the United States and the Soviet Union, it would be America who would start that war. I know Tamara saw the look of shock on my face, but I knew no one knew when or if such a war might break out—least of all Tamara's grandmother. But Tamara seemed to feel such a war was imminent, and the possibility of it hung like a consistent gray cloud over her head.

To my mind, a debate with her was foolish; we would both be grabbing at straws. So I simply said, "We can only hope such a war never happens." But I admired Tamar's silent rebellion—the lifelong fight I saw her waging as long as the Soviet Union wanted to crush the independent spirit of people like her.

Tamara now owned over half of my personal wardrobe. She paid for everything. It made me smile to know that she would look grand walking into a room, wearing an outfit I bought for myself in America but that would end up being worn by her. Clothes carried six thousand miles in my suitcase ended up in her closet in Moscow. Oh, life—you've got to love it!

I thought of my timely meeting with Bob (Robert) Robinson, the Russian from Jamaica. He was an expert engineer, and the Russian government wanted to keep a dependable, competent worker. They held onto him for more than four decades. But he was a determined man. Russia would not be able to hold him. He would find a way out, and with the help of an African official, he did.

I thought about Boris, and I knew being an artist made him somehow different. Art would always be his strength and protector and keep him shielded from a world not of his making. I have always treasured the portrait he painted of me; I'm sure a little of his spirit resides within.

I exchanged letters for a while with many of the friends I met in Moscow. When Boris wrote, he signed his letters, "Your Boris"—not "Yours truly, Boris," but "your," meaning "my" Boris.

The thought of him saying he was "my Boris" seared my heart and left me wondering if Boris and I had somehow had time to spend together, would our romance have survived the pressures of being an interracial couple?

But we were young then, and romantic notions feel good and very right when you're young. We were strong, so who knows what we could have survived? But it was apparent that our lives were meant to take separate paths.

At the airport, neither I nor Boris nor Tamara knew what to say, so we stood huddled together near the terminal building. We tried to hold on to the last fragments of our friendship, knowing the thrust of the airplane's engine would separate our worlds completely. Verbalizing a final good bye was impossible, so we promised to write.

When it was time for me to board the plane, we exchanged hasty hugs and quick kisses, and as I turned away, I felt our tightly bonded friendship slip away, removing us from all future commitments to each other, tossing us into a life exclusive of our friendship, and separating us completely by distance and circumstance.

Five years after my Russian journey, I met my husband-to-be, and reality walked in and never left. There were wedding plans, marriage vows, a new home, and the arrival, in quick succession, of three amazing children.

St. Basil's Cathedral, stands in Red Square with the Kremlin, Lenin's Mausoleum and not far away GUMS department store

CHAPTER 23

Afterthoughts

I remember the afternoon Premiere Khrushchev, who was sixty-five in 1959, came to see our fashion show. As usual, there were about four thousand Russians in the audience, and there stood the Soviet President. He looked up at the stage as the models paraded in and out, and he seemed to enjoy our presentation on his Soviet land. A photographer from *LIFE* magazine was there, and he took a picture of Khrushchev at the same moment I took my picture of the Soviet President with my little camera. The only difference in the photos was that mine was in color and *LIFE's* photo was in black and white. When the show was over, Khrushchev walked away, seemingly pleased, as his secret service men trailed behind.

But I have always felt the American National Exhibition in Moscow brought a positive interaction between Americans and Russians. Even my encounter with the Communist Chinese at the Ostankino Hotel where I was greeted with a "Hi, babe" was a breakthrough of a kind—an amazing moment. The handsome young Russian pianist who greeted me with "Take the A Train" whenever I entered the Praga Restaurant provided a lovely reminder of how music connects.

I am still amazed at how many Russians spoke English. In America, we'd never find so many Americans able to speak Russian. Perhaps our children should grow up learning a second or third language.

I had exposure to the average Russian. To have had dialogue with the average Russian was so much better than meeting any Russian government official who would already have his mind made up as to who we Americans were. But enjoying a meal, music, art, or a stroll together opened up a simple kind of commonality between people.

I visited many interesting and historic places, usually escorted by Russians I'd befriended—places like the Kremlin, GUMS Department Store, St. Basil's Museum, Red Square, the mausoleum where the body of Lenin lay, concert halls, the renowned Bolshoi Theater, Moscow University, the puppet theater, the Russian circus with Oleg Popov, the Clown, the Pushkin/Hermitage Museum, and the lovely Moskva River, where delicious sturgeon fish are caught and in which caviar is found.

But I will always cherish those nights in July and August in Moscow. The sky seemed to hang low like it was made of a heavy, deep, dark blue velvet that managed to have bright twinkling stars sprinkled throughout. As we Americans sat relaxing on the benches at Sokolniki Park, the world felt right. We viewed that beautiful Russian sky, enjoying the gentle breeze and peaceful quiet, much like the lyrics in "Moscow Nights" as sung by Vladimir Troshin. That world-famous song delighted the ears of Americans and Russians alike.

Like the matryoshka dolls that sit inside of one another, memory after memory, one after the other, comes to mind until I recall a surge of Russian moments a lifetime could never dim.

My omen did me a tremendous favor by exposing me to that moment in time when two countries stood on the brink of a war neither really wanted. Political climates change, and back then I was a black girl in Moscow who came blinded to the supposed enemy and found warm friendships that I have held in my heart through the years. Dusvedonia!

REFERENCE

http://en.wikipedia.org/wiki/File:A.S.Pushkin.jpg
Description: Alexander Pushkin
Source http://www.taday.ru/text/201360.html
Author V.A. Tropinin

www.ingramcontent.com/pod-product-compliance
Lightning Source LLC
Chambersburg PA
CBHW020523290526
45786CB00002B/737